Classic
PASTA
C·U·I·S·I·N·E

Edited by Rosemary Moon

CLB

ILLUSTRATIONS BY
CAMILLA SOPWITH, ROD FERRING AND LAWRIE TAYLOR

CLB 4362
This edition published 1995 by Colour Library Books
© 1995 Colour Library Books Ltd, Godalming, Surrey
Typeset by SX Composing, Rayleigh, Essex
All rights reserved
Printed and bound in South Africa
ISBN 1-85833-373-3

CONTENTS

INTRODUCTION

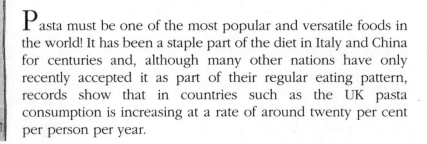

Pasta must be one of the most popular and versatile foods in the world! It has been a staple part of the diet in Italy and China for centuries and, although many other nations have only recently accepted it as part of their regular eating pattern, records show that in countries such as the UK pasta consumption is increasing at a rate of around twenty per cent per person per year.

What is Pasta?

Pasta is a very simple, natural food. When made at home it is a dough of flour and eggs, with perhaps a little olive oil added for extra flavour. The commercial dried pasta is made from the finest of all hard wheats, durum wheat, which is ground and then made into a dough with just water. Some commercial pastas are enriched with egg but, in most cases, dried pasta contains only minimal amounts of fat, making it an ideal food for those following a low fat or weight-reducing diet. (Of course served in the traditional Italian way, with plenty of butter and olive oil, the benefits of it as a diet food become a little less obvious!)

Pasta is a generic name which covers a vast number of shapes of dough, and fresh and dried varieties in many different colours. I have read that there are around six hundred different commercial pastas, but the selection available at the average supermarket is more than enough to provide plenty of variety for even the most regular of pasta eaters, and will certainly be sufficient for you when preparing the recipes in this book.

Chinese or Italian

I am not brave enough to voice an opinion as to who first came up with the idea of making and eating pasta. Of course the Italians would tell you that it is their invention, their national food and that should anyone try to say that it is not an Italian creation, then they are quite definitely out of order. It must be borne in mind, however, that when Marco Polo journeyed from Italy to China in 1270 he reported in detail on the Chinese habit of eating noodles and many people have supposed that he then brought pasta back to Italy with him. Vermicelli or noodles were nevertheless an established part of the Italian diet well before the thirteenth century, which raises more than a little doubt about the story of the travelling Italian and his booty. It is said that noodles have been eaten in China for around 6000 years, but then records in the Spaghetti Museum in Pontedassio on the Italian Riviera claim that pasta has been a staple part of the Italian diet since 5000 BC. It is said that the ancient Etruscans ate flat strips from a dough cake called *laganon*, a word of remarkable similarity to the modern word for flat strips of pasta dough – lasagne.

Pasta Doesn't Grow on Trees

I shall remain neutral in the argument about the origins of pasta, safely sitting on the fence! It must be true that for as long as man has grown wheat and has had the ability to grind it, and then to mix the resulting flour with eggs or water, he has had the potential to make pasta. Whoever made it first is irrelevant – unless you are Chinese or Italian and passionate about pasta!

One thing however, is certain. Pasta does not grow on trees! It is now several decades since Richard Dimbleby confused UK television viewers with a more than plausible April Fool showing the spaghetti harvest with many Italian workers plucking the pasta, ripened in the sun, from the branches of laden trees. The spaghetti harvest was a marvellous piece of broadcasting fun which has now been talked about, literally, for decades.

An Italian Way of Life

I know that I am going to talk far more about pasta in connection with the Italians than the Chinese, but that should not be interpreted as meaning that I am attributing the origins of pasta to the Italians and not to their rivals! It is simply that, for most of us, Italy appears to be the home of pasta as the Italians eat so much of it and many of the classic pasta recipes originate from there.

I have become convinced in my own mind that the Mediterranean sun has a great influence on people's attitude towards food. It seems that the long, hot days dictate a slower pace of life, allowing more time for people to prepare their food at home using fresh ingredients. There is no doubt at all that the pleasure associated with eating freshly cooked, home-made pasta is immeasurable against that of eating even the very best of dried pastas, so it has been traditional for centuries for the Italians to prepare their pasta at home.

Pasta is traditionally mixed and kneaded by hand, and then rolled out to a paper-like thinness on a tabletop, using an exceptionally long rolling pin made specifically for the task. The dough becomes difficult to manage for the uninitiated, but those with years of practice have a method to ensure perfect results every time. Space is the main consideration, as a large area is required to be able to roll the dough thinly without having to stop and reshape it.

The easiest pasta shapes to prepare by hand are lasagne, tagliatelle and a flat spaghetti. For many of us the art of intricate pasta shaping is something yet to be mastered!

The Advent of the Pasta Machine

I am not a great one for gadgets in the kitchen, preferring a set of sharp knives to a cupboard full of electrical wizardry that seldom gets used. I am, however, dedicated to my pasta machine to the extent that I have even clamped it to my kitchen worktable in a very prominent position. In the modern kitchen one thing that is not available is space and there simply isn't enough work surface to roll dough by hand until it is thin enough to make good, light pasta. A pasta machine which passes the dough through a series of rollers until it is ready to be shaped and cooked saves so much time and space and is, I believe, indispensable for modern cooks who wish to make their own pasta regularly in a typical modern kitchen.

I have been intrigued to read of the attitude of some of our leading chefs to pasta making in the plethora of cookbooks which now reveal the secrets of their restaurant successes. In one of my favourite books, *Leaves from The Walnut Tree* by Ann and Franco Taruschio, Franco describes how he always used to make pasta by hand but, having used standard rolling machines, he now uses an electric pasta maker which can produce almost any shape. However, he is adamant that no machine can make pasta quite as perfectly as that which is made by hand. It may then be argued that the pasta machine has caused a drop in the quality of home-made pasta. That may be so for those endowed with long rolling pins and large work surfaces, but for most of us it has opened up a whole new perspective on one of the greatest of culinary pleasures – home-made pasta cookery.

The Ancient Pasta Wars

One of the reasons why there are so many pasta shapes is because of fierce and intense competition between the main pasta makers during the Italian Renaissance in the Fifteenth and Sixteenth Centuries. They were always wanting a new shape, something different for their representatives to show, to secure an extra segment in what was a highly competitive market, even by modern standards. Of course there is no need for so many shapes and I am certain that only the largest of supermarkets or a specialist Italian grocer would ever stock more than about twenty varieties of pasta today. Pasta takes up so much room on a shelf and it would be impossible to display more than a fairly limited number of packets. I know when I had a delicatessen the maximum number of shapes that I ever stocked was ten.

The competition between pasta manufacturers is still intense, both in Italy and abroad. It is difficult to find a new sales story for a product which is basically so simple and natural. What is more interesting to me is the way in which such rivalry is now being extended to a whole new ancillary industry, that of prepared pasta sauces. Certainly in the UK this is one of the fastest growing sectors of the food market and competition is very hot. However, as pasta is such a natural product I think it is important to ensure that the sauce or sauce base that you purchase, if indeed you do so, is as natural as possible with no additives. When I buy such products I always ignore the leading brand names and go for the all natural sauces clearly labelled as additive free, or an Italian produced sauce base, again with no extra E-numbers.

Fresh or Dried

You might well expect me to say here that fresh pasta is always better than dried, and that the latter should only be resorted to in moments of utter desperation, or when the last egg in your kitchen has been used and the shops are all shut. Well, that's not the case at all!

I have to say that I do think home-made pasta is always better than bought, and that it is immeasurably superior to commercially prepared fresh pasta. I always find the fresh pasta available in supermarkets too thick, and consequently heavy to eat. Fresh pasta in sealed packets will keep for about 4-5 days and many people do like to keep a packet or two in the freezer for emergency use. However, I always choose to use a dried pasta if I don't have time to make my own, as I actually prefer the texture of the dried product.

Having stated my reservations, there is no doubt that fresh pasta is becoming a very popular line in most large supermarkets, where more and more colours and shapes are being introduced. One supermarket near me sells fresh tomato and black pastas, the latter being coloured with squid ink. I have noticed that the thinner shapes such as spaghetti are the most popular.

There's Dried & Dried

There are basically two types of pastas – *pasta all'uovo* or *pasta fatta in casa*, that is home-made egg pasta, or *pasta secca*, the commercial dried pasta made from a flour and water paste. You may well consider that all dried pastas must be the same, but there is a world of difference in quality between them and you definitely get what you pay for when it comes to pasta. Most supermarkets sell their own brand and there are plenty of proprietary products which are very well known. All are reasonable, but they simply do not compare to the Italian dried pastas which are available in delicatessens, specialist food shops and even in some of the flag-ship stores of the major supermarket chains. The Italian pasta has a much firmer texture and is more akin to a home-made pasta when cooked.

I recently met up with a cousin whom I had not seen for some time at a wedding. She said that she had read a piece that I had written expressing the same views on the merits of Italian dried pasta as I have just expounded. Since then, Andrea has bought nothing except the Italian product and has been delighted with the quality and the improved flavour and texture. (I always feel that I am winning when the family start to take notice!)

A Limited Selection

The only drawback to making your own pasta is that you are somewhat limited in the number of shapes that you can produce. They are mostly flat, folded or rolled as they have to come from a flat sheet of dough. I make more tagliatelle at home than anything else – it is easy as it is one of the three 'shapes' on the pasta machine. The basic dough is rolled into strips or lasagne, and then there are two extra sets of cutters on the standard machine for tagliatelle and flat spaghetti. The lasagne may be cut and made into ravioli or cannelloni, but there is certainly no way of making macaroni or pasta shells. However, small rectangles of pasta may be pinched together in the centre, having been cut with a wheel cutter, to form farfalle, pasta butterflies or bows.

All Shapes and Sizes

Although I am convinced that some of the six hundred names attributed to pasta shapes must be duplicates, there is no doubt at all that there are literally hundreds of different varieties of pasta. I know that there are some duplicates because there is one very famous example. The town of Bologna in the Emilia-Romagna region is *the* gastronomic centre of northern Italy. It has many claims to fame in the culinary world and is the very heart of the Lambrusco grape growing region. It is renowned for its meat sauces and also for one specific type of pasta, tagliatelle. Like spaghetti, it is an ideal shape for mixing with a smooth sauce, becoming evenly coated with the delicious juices and granules of ingredients. However, just down the motorway in the Italian capital, tagliatelle, the beloved speciality of Bologna, is widely referred to as fettucini, a favourite pasta of the Romans. I suppose it's a bit like the confusion between the English and Scots over swedes and turnips!

Different Shapes for Different Dishes

I always divide pastas into five main groups, according to how they are to be cooked and served:

Pastas for coating with a smooth sauce is the most popular group. It includes spaghetti, tagliatelle and all the various thicknesses of vermicelli. When eating Italian, do as the Italians do! They would never sit down to a mound of spaghetti with a dollop of Bolognese sauce atop the mountain! Even if the dish is brought to the table in such a way, the sauce is tossed into the pasta before serving, coating the strands evenly to produce a dish of wonderful flavours. Try it – it's so much better than the mountaineering approach!

Surprise Pastas is my name for the shapes which can harbour the good bits of a sauce! I include shells, penne, large macaroni and farfalle and the countless other shapes that have recesses to catch prawns, pine nuts, diced vegetables and globules of dressing, giving surprise mouthfuls of tangy flavour in the middle of a dish.

Pastas for stuffing should contain their filling during the cooking process. The two most popular varieties are ravioli and cannelloni. Stuffed ravioli are available ready prepared, the fresh varieties being a great improvement over the canned in tomato sauce, which is a travesty of good Italian cooking. However, making ravioli at home allows for far more creative fillings. Cannelloni should be crisp on top, either from grilling or from baking in a very hot oven, whilst remaining tender and moist underneath.

Pastas for baking are usually boiled before being included in a composite dish to be baked in the oven, or *al forno*. The most obvious is lasagne, the broad sheets of pasta so easily produced by a domestic pasta machine. However, large macaroni and penne may also be baked and are both especially attractive when lined up neatly to form a layer in a dish that is to be cut when served.

Small pastas for soup are known collectively as pastini. They are tiny so that they will cook quickly and blend in well with other ingredients in the soup, yet remain easy to eat with a spoon. Pastini are also useful for sweet pasta dishes.

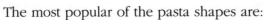

The most popular of the pasta shapes are:

Spaghetti, long fine strands of pasta, is without doubt, the most popular shape in the world. It is available in different thicknesses and I like to use a fine spaghetti, the finest of which is called spaghettini. Italian spaghetti has the best texture.

Vermicelli is one of the Italian names for the pasta that would be referred to as fine noodles in China. Another Italian name is capellini and the very finest variety is called *capelli d'angelo*, or angel's hair. Vermicelli are used in soups or broken up in sweet dishes, and may also be used to create pasta nests which are deep-fried and then used as baskets for serving designer savoury dishes.

Tagliatelle is probably my favourite pasta. It is thin ribbons of dough which should be only about 6mm/¼ inch thick and it is an excellent vehicle for any number of sauces. I think it is easier to eat than spaghetti as, being flat, it cannot slide off a fork so easily!

Lasagne are the broad sheets of pasta most frequently used for baking in a dish of meat, fish or vegetable sauce which is then usually topped with a white sauce and grated cheese. Home-made lasagne is always flat but dried lasagne can be bought with a decorative ruffled edge. Lasagne should be boiled before it is baked and this is best done a few sheets at a time – any more and the pasta will stick together in the pan. Easy-cook lasagne is available which requires no pre-cooking, but it bears a remarkable resemblance to cardboard when compared to the fresh pasta.

Cannelloni tubes are easily made at home from a basic lasagne, then par-boiled and dried over a broom handle before stuffing (that is, a broom handle kept specifically for pasta making duties, and not used at other times for beating carpets etc!). If buying dried cannelloni shells, check the packet carefully before purchasing to ensure that there are no broken tubes underneath the top layer of pasta. A broken cannelloni shell is of little use to anyone.

Ravioli are little parcels of pasta, usually with a savoury filling. Ravioli tins are available, whereby a sheet of pasta is laid over the tin and filling is added where the recesses are marked. A second sheet of pasta is then laid over the first and a rolling pin is passed over the top. This forces the filling down into the recesses of the ravioli moulds and seals the pasta sheets together around the filling whilst cutting the dough into squares over the perforations of the tin. This produces small ravioli which are ideal for cooking in a soup. Ravioli are always served in a sauce.

Tortellini are small, filled pastas which may be home-made, although the folding requires some skill to keep the filling enclosed. They are available dried and are ideal store-cupboard food, for the occasion when you really do not want to cook. Tortellini should be served in a sauce, otherwise they are dry. Legend says that the shape of this pasta is modelled on Venus's navel – I wonder how she would have responded to the fact that some people now refer to tortellini as pasta dumplings?

Pastini is the collective name for tiny pasta shapes suitable for cooking in soup, or *in brodo*. Some of the most inventive shapes are within this group – there are alphabet letters, space invaders, tiny flowers and all sorts of cartoon characters. Many pastini are sold ready-cooked in a sauce as children's food for serving on toast, but this is definitely not a traditional presentation.

Fusilli are pasta spirals and are marvellous for catching little globules of sauce within their coils. Their attractive shapes also makes them an ideal pasta for serving cold in salads. Fusilli was one of the first shapes to be available as tri-coloured pasta, dried from the supermarket shelf. The colours are usually yellow, green and red; egg, spinach and tomato.

Farfalle are another decorative shape, this time resembling bows. Sauce collects in the middle, in the ruches, so this is another pasta to serve with tasty, savoury sauces. I think that farfalle make a particularly attractive starter.

Conchiglie or shells come in various sizes, from pastini right up to large shells which may be stuffed and served as a starter. The medium-sized variety are a popular shape as they too trap mouthfuls of delicious sauce to create surprise bursts of flavour.

Macaroni is available in two types – straight and elbow, the latter having a slight kink in the middle. It is said that the Holy Roman Emperor Frederick II was so fond of this shape that he named it macaroni after *marcus* – the divine dish. Macaroni comes in various thicknesses but it always has a hole through the middle. I used to sell long macaroni, the length of spaghetti, when I had my delicatessen and it was very popular. It can be used to line a pudding basin, resembling an old-fashioned beehive, which can then be filled and baked or steamed. However, I have not seen long macaroni now for several years, and that which is generally available is referred to as short-cut.

Penne is another of my favourite pastas, being tubes cut on the slant of about 1.25cm/½ inch diameter when dry, and which trap mouthfuls of flavour when mixed with a sauce. Penne are available plain or lightly ribbed – I prefer the latter.

Rigatoni is another tube variety of pasta, this time straight cut and almost always ribbed. The name is derived from the Italian word *riga*, which means line.

Cappelletti are one of the few shapes which can be made easily at home. They are more attractive with a fluted edge, so cut them out of a strip of dough using a fluted petit-four cutter. To achieve the cap shape, press the dough into the palm of one hand with the opposite thumb, turning the thumb gently to form the indentation.

Ruoti are pasta wheels and are available in various sizes. They are an attractive shape to use in soups or cold, in pasta salads.

Gnocchi, like conchiglie, also resemble small shells and are an excellent shape for salads and hot dishes where there are tasty morsels to be trapped within the pasta.

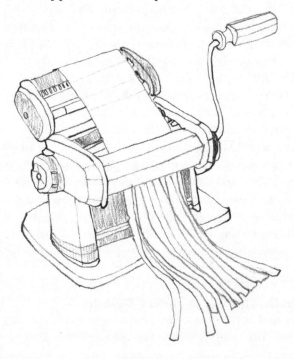

Pasta Extrusion

Many of the shapes described here are extruded through a machine which forces the dough into shape under a certain amount of pressure. There are domestic versions of pasta extruders, one of which is an attachment for a table mixer. These, however, tend to be slow and laboured in their task and may take almost half an hour to extrude sufficient pasta to feed four or six people, the dough for which must be of just the right consistency. On balance, and I have owned both types of machine, I prefer the pasta roller, despite its more limited potential for producing shapes.

The Basic Pasta Dough

Pasta dough is simply a mixture of flour and eggs, with a little water or olive oil if necessary for flavour, or to bind the dough together. My basic recipe for four to six people is

> 460g/1lb strong plain white flour
> 4 eggs, lightly beaten
> Olive oil or water, if necessary

Place the flour in a large mixing bowl and make a well in the centre. Add the beaten eggs and bring the mixture together, using first a fork and then your fingers. Add a few drops of oil or water if the dough is too dry. Gather the dough up into a ball, then knead it with the heel of your hand until it is smooth, shiny and no longer sticky. Cover the dough in plastic wrap and leave it in a cool place to rest for 30 minutes if you are to roll it by hand. If you are going to be using a pasta machine you can press on with the rolling and shaping of the pasta straight away. Allowing the dough to rest helps to prevent it from springing back out of shape during rolling by hand.

I generally use size 2 eggs when making pasta and find that just the four eggs are sufficient to make the dough without any extra oil. However, all flours vary in the amount of liquid that they will absorb, so it is as well to be prepared to add a little extra moisture if required.

A Drier Dough Gives Better Results

The easiest mistake to make when producing home-made pasta is to make the dough too wet. Although it will feel good to handle it will not cut readily in a pasta machine and the strands will have more of a tendency to stick together during cooking. The dough should be dry but not quite crumbly. You should not require much additional flour on the work surface to prevent the dough from sticking and you may find that you have to pass it through the rollers of a pasta machine twice on setting one to achieve a smooth sheet of pasta without splits. However, after the initial rolling, the dough will be easy to handle and will fall readily into strands if cut by machine into tagliatelle or spaghetti.

Salt in the Dough or Salt in the Water?

Many pasta recipes call for a good pinch of salt to be added to the flour before the dough is mixed. I am of the school of thought that says this has a tendency to make the dough tough, and that it is better to add the salt to the water when cooking the pasta. This is especially true when making wholewheat pasta.

Fine Flour for Wholewheat Varieties

I always think that commercial wholewheat pasta is wooden in texture and totally lacking in flavour. However, home-made wholewheat is delicious and totally unlike the commercial alternative. To make a good dough it is essential that you use a fine wholemeal flour – bread flour is not suitable as it has too much bran in too large flakes which will cause the dough to tear. I use the same quantities of flour and eggs as for the basic egg dough, but always add one tablespoon of olive oil with the eggs. This helps to start the binding of the dough and more can be added if necessary. Wholewheat pasta tends to be a little drier than the egg variety, so the dough should be carefully monitored during mixing.

Musical Pasta?

Pasta verde is not an opera, it is a green dough coloured and flavoured with spinach! The quantities of flour and eggs are slightly different to those for the standard doughs as some spinach purée has to be incorporated into the mixture with the eggs. A good basic recipe is

280g/10oz strong plain white flour
2 eggs, lightly beaten
120g/4oz cooked spinach, finely chopped or puréed
Olive oil, if necessary

Sieve the flour into a mixing bowl and make a well in the centre. Beat together the eggs and the spinach purée and add them to the flour. Mix with a fork and then with your hands until the dough can be gathered into a ball. Add a little oil if the mixture is too dry and a little flour if it is too wet. Knead lightly, until the dough is smooth and shiny and the spinach has evenly coloured it. Cover and rest for 30 minutes before rolling by hand or machine.

The Technicolour Cook

Once you start making pasta you will want to experiment with all sorts of colourings and flavours. Finely chopped herbs produce an attractive green fleck in yellow egg pasta, whilst a dramatic yellow colour may be produced by adding a few teaspoons of saffron or turmeric infusion – the former has the more subtle flavour. Beetroot and tomato purées both produce red doughs whilst carrot gives a good orange colour. Perhaps the most dramatic of all is black pasta which is coloured with squid ink. It has little flavour but looks stunning when served with shellfish in a cream sauce.

Rules for Cooking Perfect Pasta

There are a few basic guidelines to follow to produce perfect pasta, which apply to both dried and fresh varieties. They are:

* Always cook pasta in a large pan in plenty of boiling salted water. This will help to prevent it from sticking together during cooking.

* Do not overcook pasta. It should be tender but still firm, with a little bite. This is called *al dente*. Fresh pasta will take only a minute or so to cook, and is ready when it floats to the top of the pan.

* Rinse pasta in boiling or cold water after cooking, depending on how it is to be used. This helps to wash away any surplus starch.

* Do not drain cooked pasta too vigorously: give the colander a brief, firm shake, then leave it to drain. Shake too much and the pasta will stick together.

* When boiling lasagne, only add a few sheets at a time to the pan, then lay the par-boiled sheets on clean tea towels until required.

Fun for All the Family

Pasta making is great fun and even the youngest child who wants to help in the kitchen can enjoy turning the handle of the pasta machine. I talk to more and more people who tell me that pasta making is now a family activity with everyone involved, and enjoying it. It is not complicated and is a good thing to start would-be-cooks on in the kitchen, having far more relevance to our modern way of life than the fairy cakes that I started baking as a child.

After teaching a cookery holiday for 10-14 year olds I was interested to read the questionnaires that were filled in by the participants at the end of the week. The children were of very mixed culinary ability when they arrived and one little girl of ten, who had done next-to-no cooking before the holiday, commented that making pasta for the first evening's supper had been her favourite thing as she had never cooked a real meal before – an excellent way to start!

Oriental Pastas

Although Chinese egg noodles are very similar to the Italian egg pasta, there are other oriental pastas which are very different indeed. These include rice noodles which are long spaghetti-like strands. They are seldom cut and are sold folded back on themselves in very long lengths. Some rice noodles are as thin as vermicelli and these are most often used as a thickening for clear Chinese soups. The Chinese developed rice noodles as wheat is only grown in the north of the country and rice is the staple food in all other areas.

I have commented before that cellophane noodles are not an oriental attempt at recycling unwanted packaging! They are actually made from a paste of ground mung beans and are virtually transparent, which has lead to their unusual name. Cellophane noodles are very fine and are soaked before being added to stir-frys; they do not require boiling before they are used.

The last of the oriental noodles in common use is Japanese menrui. Menrui is actually a general name for noodles made from either wheat or buckwheat. They are sold in varying thicknesses and are usually boiled. Menrui are, however, cooked to a much softer texture than the *al dente* of the standard egg noodles.

All pasta is fun to cook. Try making your own dough, and discover the true delights of this simple and versatile food.

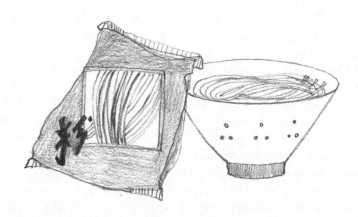

SOUPS

For many centuries most meals were soups in one form or another. This was for the simple reason that the only real cooking facility available in any home, even those of the wealthy, was an iron pot hanging over an open fire. These soups were the original one-pot meals. In the households of the wealthy the meal would have been more akin to a stew with plenty of meat and vegetables but in the poorer homes, where the resources and ingredients were much less, the meal became watered down into a soup. Different vegetables, cereals or grains were used to thicken the soups and give more substance to the meal, according to the cuisine of the area. Root vegetables and eventually potatoes were popular thickening agents in many countries, as well as grains such as pearl barley, rice or lentils. In China and Italy, however, it was pasta or noodles that were used, to thicken the soups and to add body to them, and this is still the case today.

The Changing Role of Soup

From playing the major part in almost every meal in every culture, the function of soups has changed dramatically and become almost watered-down to a supporting role to the main course, an appetiser to set the scene for what is to come. Thus the majority of soups that are enjoyed today are thinner and less substantial than their illustrious ancestors, being lighter and less filling.

Pasta in Soup

The very nature of modern-day soups demands that you don't attempt to cook large pasta shells or spirals in them. They would look ungainly, be much larger than the majority of the other ingredients and would also be more than little difficult to eat elegantly with a spoon! There are a great number of small pasta shapes available specifically for soups, which cook quickly and are easy to eat. These range from cartoon characters and alphabet letters (doubtless to encourage children to eat their food by making it fun) to tiny shells and other, more sophisticated shapes. As there is such a variety of pasta for soup most of the shapes do not have their own names but are known by the general term of *pastini* or *pasta in brodo*.

Quick to Cook

I feel that you would need the patience of a saint to fashion even a one-egg dough mix into pastini for soup! It is therefore much easier to buy these little pasta shapes in a dried form, and to keep them in the store-cupboard for use as required. As the shapes are so small they are quick to cook – most dried pasta shapes have to be boiled for 10-12 minutes but pastini are generally cooked within 4-5 minutes.

Two Classics from the Two Great Pasta Nations

China and Italy, the two great pasta nations, each have a classic pasta soup that is an integral part of their national cuisine. In Italy it is Minestrone, which would be little more than a tomato soup without the addition of broken spaghetti to help thicken the brew, and the classic Chicken Noodle is one of the most popular of Chinese soups. When made with a fresh and nutritious chicken stock, it provides an excellent light meal for invalids and those without much appetite.

Hearty Soups for Cold Winter's Days

Most pasta soups are really throw-backs to the days of one-pot eating: they are richly flavoured, hearty meals that almost have the consistency of a stew (although usually without meat) and can be served as a complete meal with the simple addition of a loaf of fresh, crusty bread. This chapter contains recipes from different countries, all of which feature pasta. The Spiced Fried Soup is a classic dish from Indonesia, whereas the Cabbage & Pasta Soup is based on the French passion for cabbage dishes.

Surprise Parcels in the Soup

No, not a repetition of "Waiter, there's a fly in my soup!" I am referring to the tradition of serving more substantial mouthfuls in a well-flavoured stock or consommé, in the same way as the Chinese would serve a wonton soup with little savoury parcels in a clear broth. I have included recipes for Ravioli Soup, the Italian answer to the Chinese wonton dish which is served in a tomato-flavoured stock, and a Meatball Soup, which includes baked meatballs in a tasty liquor containing pastini.

MINESTRONE

There are so many recipes for the classic Italian soup of minestrone. This recipe has a rich, pesto-like mayonnaise added as a delicious garnish.

Serves 4-6

INGREDIENTS
120g/4oz dried haricot beans, soaked overnight
2 tbsps olive oil
120g/4oz piece bacon
1 carrot, diced
2 medium-sized potatoes, diced
60g/2oz peas (shelled, fresh or frozen)
½ courgette, diced
120g/4oz pasta shells

Sauce
10 fresh basil leaves
15g/½oz pine nuts
1 egg yolk
1 clove garlic, finely chopped
150ml/¼ pint olive oil
Salt and freshly ground black pepper
30g/1oz finely grated Cheddar or Parmesan

Rinse and drain the beans. Heat the olive oil in a large saucepan and gently sauté the beans and bacon for 1 minute. Add plenty of water and cook for about 45 minutes until the beans are cooked.

To make the sauce, crush together the basil leaves and the pine nuts. Add the egg and garlic. Gradually whisk in the olive oil until the sauce thickens like mayonnaise. Season with salt and pepper. Add the grated cheese to the sauce, stir well and set aside.

Add the carrot, potatoes and peas to the beans, cook for a further 15 minutes and then add the courgette and pasta and cook for a final 15 minutes. Remove the piece of bacon and serve the soup accompanied by the sauce.

CHICKEN SOUP WITH VERMICELLI

This light chicken soup is perfect as part of a Mediterranean-style meal but may also be used as a nutritious dish to tempt anyone who has lost their appetite.

Serves 4

INGREDIENTS

45g/1½oz butter
1 carrot, finely sliced
1 bay leaf
1 onion, finely sliced
1kg/2¼lbs chicken carcass (bones and meat)
½ leek (white part only), finely sliced
Salt and freshly ground black pepper
60g/2oz vermicelli
2 tbsps freshly chopped chives

Heat the butter and gently fry the carrot and bay leaf for 2 minutes. Add the onion and continue cooking for 2 minutes. Add the chicken carcass, roughly chopped, and fry, shaking the pan, for a few minutes. Pour over enough water to cover the ingredients. Stir in the leek and season with salt and pepper. Cook over a moderate heat for 45 minutes, adding extra water if necessary. Strain the contents of the pan through a fine sieve, reserving only the stock. Pour the stock into a clean saucepan, bring to the boil and add the vermicelli. Cook for approximately 2 minutes, then serve, sprinkled with the chopped chives.

CHICKEN AND VEGETABLE SOUP WITH CURRY

*This is a spicy Thai recipe for chicken soup and is delicious!
Be careful when seasoning the soup – macadamia nuts
can be very salty and little or no extra seasoning
may be required.*

Serves 4

INGREDIENTS
1kg/2¼lbs chicken pieces
1 tbsp curry leaves
2 tbsps oil
4 shallots, roughly chopped
1 clove garlic, crushed
1 red or green chilli, seeded and
  finely chopped
2 tsps mild curry powder
1 small piece fresh root ginger,
  grated
30g/1oz chopped macadamia
  nuts

90g/3oz Chinese noodles,
  softened for 5 minutes in hot
  water
2 courgettes, diced
Juice of 1 lime
Salt

Garnish
Thin slices of lime

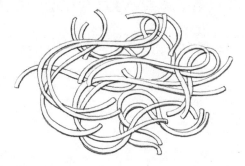

Place the chicken and curry leaves in a deep pan and cover with water. Simmer, partially covered, for 30-45 minutes or until the chicken is tender. Skim the fat or scum from the top of the liquid while the chicken cooks.

Heat the oil in a small pan and add the shallots and garlic. Cook until slightly softened. Add the chilli, curry powder and ginger and cook for 2 minutes. Add the nuts and set aside.

When the chicken is cooked, remove it from the liquid and allow to cool. Strain and reserve the stock. Remove the skin and bones from the chicken and cut the meat into small pieces. Add the chicken and cooked onions, garlic and spices to the strained stock in the rinsed-out pan. Bring to the boil and add the noodles and courgettes. Simmer to cook the noodles completely and add lime juice and salt, if necessary. Garnish with lime slices and serve.

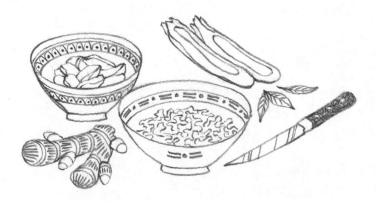

SPICED FRIED SOUP

This soup is so substantial that it is a complete meal in itself.
It is a classic dish of Indonesia.

Serves 4

INGREDIENTS

4-8 tbsps oil
1 clove garlic
460g/1lb chicken breast, skinned, boned and cut into small pieces
225g/8oz tofu, drained and cut into 2.5cm/1 inch cubes
60g/2oz raw cashew nuts
4 shallots, roughly chopped
1 carrot, very thinly sliced
90g/3oz mangetout
60g/2oz Chinese noodles, soaked for 5 minutes in hot water and drained thoroughly
1.4 litres/2½ pints vegetable or chicken stock
Juice of 1 lime
¼ tsp turmeric
2 curry leaves
1 tsp grated fresh root ginger
1 tbsp soy sauce
Salt and freshly ground black pepper

Heat 2-3 tbsps of the oil in a wok or large frying pan. Add the garlic and cook until brown. Remove the garlic from the pan and discard it. Add the chicken pieces and cook in the oil until they begin to brown. Remove the pieces using a slotted spoon and drain well on absorbent kitchen paper. Add a little more oil and cook the tofu until lightly brown. Remove and drain well. Add the cashews and cook, stirring constantly, until toasted. Remove and drain well. Add a little more oil and fry the shallots and carrots until lightly browned. Stir in the mangetout and cook for 1 minute. Remove from the pan and drain.

Heat the oil in the wok until it is very hot, adding any remaining from the original amount. Add the drained noodles and cook quickly until brown on one side. Turn over and brown the other side. Lower the heat and pour in the stock. Stir in the lime juice, turmeric, curry leaves, ginger, soy sauce and seasoning. Cover and simmer gently for 10 minutes, stirring occasionally to prevent the noodles from sticking. Add the fried ingredients and heat through for 5 minutes. Season to taste and serve immediately.

LAMB AND NOODLE SOUP

Most Chinese soups are light and thin, but this one is quite substantial. Slice the lamb very thinly to ensure that it cooks through quickly. Transparent noodles may be cut with a sharp knife if they are difficult to break.

Serves 4

INGREDIENTS
120g/4oz transparent noodles
6 Chinese dried mushrooms, soaked for 15 minutes in warm water
700ml/1¼ pints lamb stock, skimmed
175g/6oz lamb fillet, thinly sliced
1 tbsp soy sauce
Few drops chilli sauce
Salt and freshly ground black pepper

Break the transparent noodles into small pieces and cook them in boiling, salted water for 20 seconds. Rinse them in fresh water and set aside to drain. Cook the mushrooms in boiling, lightly salted water for 15 minutes, rinse them in fresh water and set aside to drain. Cut the mushrooms into thin slices.

Heat the lamb stock in a saucepan and add the lamb, mushrooms, soy sauce and a few drops of chilli sauce. Season with salt and pepper and simmer gently for 15 minutes. Stir in the drained noodles and simmer for just long enough for the noodles to heat through. Serve immediately.

BEEF AND NOODLE SOUP

This is a rich, filling soup, deliciously flavoured with marinated beef.

Serves 4

Ingredients
225g/8oz fillet of beef
1 clove garlic, chopped
1 spring onion, chopped
2 tbsps soy sauce
Salt and freshly ground black pepper
225g/8oz fresh noodles or fine tagliatelle
Few drops sesame oil
700ml/1¼ pints beef stock
Few drops chilli sauce
1 tbsp freshly chopped chives

Cut the beef into thin slices. Sprinkle the chopped garlic and spring onion over the meat with the soy sauce and season with salt and pepper. Marinate the meat for 15 minutes. Cook the noodles in boiling, salted water to which a few drops of sesame oil have been added, until tender but still firm. Rinse the noodles and set aside to drain. Bring the beef stock to the boil and add the beef and the marinade. Simmer gently for 10 minutes. Stir in the noodles, season with a few drops of chilli sauce and simmer for just long enough to heat the noodles through. Serve garnished with chives.

THICK CHICKEN NOODLE SOUP

A very meaty and substantial soup. Add more water or stock for a thinner and less filling soup.

Serves 6

INGREDIENTS
1 chicken weighing about
    1.4kg/3lbs
2 carrots, chopped
1 leek, sliced
60g/2oz vermicelli noodles
1 tbsp freshly chopped mixed
    herbs
Salt and freshly ground black
    pepper

Joint the chicken and place the pieces in a large pan with sufficient water to cover the meat. Add the chopped vegetables and bring to the boil. Cover the pan and simmer for 1 hour.

Strain the stock and return it to the pan. Bone the chicken, shred the meat and return it to the stock. Bring to the boil and add the vermicelli, herbs and seasonings. Simmer for a further 15 minutes, adding extra water if necessary. Season to taste and serve.

CHICKPEA SOUP

This is a substantial soup, suitable for the coldest of winter days. Liquidise the soup before adding the pasta, if preferred.

Serves 4

INGREDIENTS
200g/7oz dried chickpeas
3 tbsps olive oil
2 cloves garlic
340g/12oz plum tomatoes, chopped
700ml/1¼ pints water
1 tbsp fresh basil leaves
1 chicken stock cube
Salt and freshly ground black pepper
150g/5oz small pasta shapes for soup
45g/1½oz Parmesan cheese, grated

Soak the chickpeas overnight in enough water to cover them by 2.5cm/1 inch. Discard the water and place the chickpeas in a large, heavy pan with a similar amount of fresh water. Bring to the boil and simmer, covered, for about 1 hour, until the chickpeas are tender, ensuring that they do not boil dry.

Heat the olive oil in a heavy pan, and sauté the garlic cloves. When browned, remove and discard the garlic. Add the tomatoes and their juice, the water and basil, and cook for 20 minutes. Add the drained chickpeas, crumbled stock cube, and salt and pepper to taste. Stir well and simmer for a further 10 minutes.

Return the soup to the boil and add the pasta, then cook, stirring frequently, for 10 minutes. Mix in half of the Parmesan cheese. Adjust the seasoning, and serve immediately, with the remaining Parmesan cheese sprinkled on top.

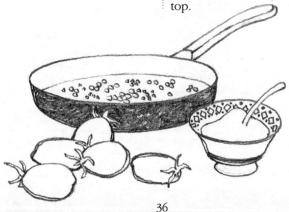

CABBAGE AND PASTA SOUP

Cabbage soups are very popular in France, but this one has a very definite Italian flavour.

Serves 4

INGREDIENTS
6 leaves white cabbage
150g/5oz small pasta shells
1 rasher streaky bacon, cut into small dice
1 clove garlic, chopped
1 tbsp olive oil
850ml/1½ pints chicken stock
Salt and freshly ground black pepper

Cut the cabbage into thin shreds. To do this, roll the leaves into cigar shapes and cut with a very sharp knife. Heat the olive oil in a large pan and fry the garlic, bacon and cabbage together for 2 minutes. Add the stock, season with salt and pepper and cook over a moderate heat for 30 minutes. Add the pasta to the soup after it has been cooking for 15 minutes. Check the seasoning and serve.

TOMATO SOUP

A tomato soup with a difference. Use two tablespoons of horseradish sauce if grated horseradish is not available.

Serves 4-6

INGREDIENTS

30g/1oz butter or margarine
1 small onion, chopped
1 small green pepper, seeded
and chopped
1 tbsp flour
1 litre/1¾ pints brown stock, or
water plus 2 beef stock cubes
460g/1lb tomatoes, chopped
2 tbsps tomato purée
Salt and freshly ground black
pepper
120g/4oz short-cut macaroni
1 tbsp grated horseradish

Garnish
2 tbsps soured cream
1 tbsp freshly chopped parsley

Heat the butter in a pan, add the onion and green pepper, then cover and cook for 5 minutes. Add the flour and stir. Cook for 1 minute then add the stock, tomatoes and tomato purée. Bring to the boil then simmer for 15 minutes.

Blend the soup until smooth in a liquidiser or food processor then press it through a sieve. Return it to the pan, and season with salt and pepper to taste. Add the macaroni 10 minutes before serving. Simmer and stir occasionally. Stir in the horseradish and garnish with soured cream and parsley. Serve immediately.

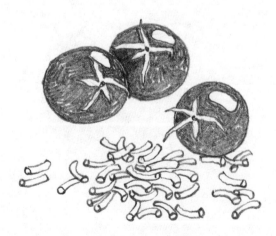

BEAN SOUP

Not so much a soup, more a meal in a dish!

Serves 4-6

INGREDIENTS

425g/15oz can red kidney beans
60g/2oz bacon, rinded and
 chopped
1 stick celery, chopped
1 small onion, chopped
1 clove garlic, crushed
1 tbsp freshly chopped parsley
1 tbsp freshly chopped basil
90g/3oz canned plum tomatoes,
 seeded and chopped
1 litre/1¾ pints water
1 chicken stock cube
Salt and freshly ground black
 pepper
120g/4oz wholewheat pasta

Place the kidney beans, bacon, celery, onion, garlic, parsley, basil, tomatoes and water in a large pan. Bring to the boil and add the stock cube and salt and pepper to taste. Cover and simmer for about 1½ hours. Return the soup to the boil and add the pasta, stirring well. Stir frequently until the pasta is cooked but still firm – about 10 minutes. Season and serve immediately.

PRAWN AND NOODLE SOUP

This is a hearty, satisfying fish soup. The tofu provides plenty of protein and makes the soup almost a complete meal in itself.

Serves 4

INGREDIENTS
1 small bunch spring onions
175g/6oz raw, unpeeled prawns
1 bay leaf
1 small piece fresh root ginger, peeled and left whole
2 cloves garlic, peeled and left whole
1 tbsp crushed coriander seeds
1¼ litres/2 pints water
¼ tsp turmeric
1 red chilli seeded and cut into very thin, short strips
280ml/½ pint coconut milk
175g/6oz Chinese noodles, soaked 5 minutes in hot water
225g/8oz tofu, drained and cut into 1.25cm/½ inch cubes
175g/6oz bean sprouts
Lemon juice
Salt

Cut the green tops off the spring onions and set aside. Combine the white part of the onions, prawns, bay leaf, ginger, garlic, coriander seeds and water in a deep saucepan. Bring to the boil and simmer just until the prawns turn pink. Remove the prawns with a slotted spoon and peel them. Return the skins to the stock in the pan, chop the prawns and set them aside. Simmer the stock for a further 15-20 minutes. Strain and return to the rinsed-out pan. Add the turmeric, chilli pepper and coconut milk. Bring to the boil, add the noodles and simmer until completely cooked. Slice the green tops of the spring onions thinly and add to the stock with the tofu, bean sprouts, lemon juice and prawns. Add salt to taste and simmer until all the ingredients are hot.

CURRIED MEATBALL AND NOODLE SOUP

Oriental noodle soups often contain meatballs. Chop the shallots for the meatballs very finely to prevent the meatballs from breaking up during cooking.

Serves 4

INGREDIENTS
Meatballs
225g/8oz finely minced lean beef
2 shallots, finely chopped
Pinch of salt and pepper
1 tsp cornflour
1 egg white

Soup
2 tbsps oil
3 shallots, finely chopped
1 clove garlic, crushed
1 tbsp curry powder
1 carrot, peeled and sliced
1.4 litres/2½ pints stock
Salt and freshly ground black
  pepper
90g/3oz Chinese noodles
Half a head Chinese leaves,
  shredded

Garnish
Chopped macadamia nuts
Coriander leaves

Combine all the ingredients for the meatballs and mix well. Shape into 2.5cm/1 inch balls and chill until ready to use.

Heat the oil in a heavy-based saucepan and add the shallots, garlic and curry powder. Cook until the shallots soften. Add the carrots and stock. Partially cover the pan and bring the stock to the boil. Allow to simmer for 15 minutes then add the meatballs. Simmer for 5-7 minutes or until the meatballs are cooked. Add the Chinese noodles and cook about 5 minutes or until just tender. Add salt, pepper and the Chinese leaves. Cook for a further 5 minutes until the leaves are tender-crisp. Spoon the soup into individual bowls and garnish with chopped nuts and whole coriander leaves.

MINESTRA

This is a substantial variation on the classic Italian soup Minestrone. I particularly like the spinach in it.

Serves 4-6

INGREDIENTS

1 onion
1 carrot
1 stick celery
2 tbsps olive oil
1.7 litres/3 pints water
Salt and freshly ground black
  pepper
225g/8oz fresh spinach
2 tomatoes
120g/4oz short-cut macaroni
2 cloves garlic, crushed
2 tbsps freshly chopped parsley
1 tsp freshly chopped rosemary
60g/2oz Parmesan cheese, grated

Cut the onion, carrot and celery into thick matchsticks. Heat the oil in a large, heavy pan, and fry the vegetable strips until just browning, stirring occasionally. Add the water, salt and pepper, and simmer for 20 minutes. Meanwhile, wash the spinach leaves and cut them into shreds. Add to the soup and cook for 10 minutes. Peel the tomatoes and chop them roughly, removing the seeds. Add the tomatoes, macaroni, garlic, parsley and rosemary to the soup, and simmer a further 10 minutes. Adjust the seasoning. Serve with grated Parmesan cheese.

RAVIOLI SOUP

The ravioli makes surprise parcels of flavour in a clear soup.
The secret of success is to use a good homemade stock.

Serves 4

INGREDIENTS
225g/8oz pasta dough (see page 19)
3 slices Parma ham, cut into very thin strips
1 litre/1¾ pints chicken stock
30g/1oz butter
1 egg, beaten
1 sprig tarragon, leaves stripped off and cut into thin strips
2 tbsps single cream
Nutmeg
Salt and freshly ground black pepper

Prepare the pasta dough and roll it very thinly, either with a rolling pin or by passing it through a pasta machine. Cut it into rectangles. Place a little Parma ham and butter on one half of each piece, then brush the edges of the dough with the beaten egg. Fold each rectangle in half to form a square and pinch the edges well with your fingers to seal. Cut into neat squares or various shapes using a ravioli cutter and pinch the edges to seal, if necessary.

Bring the stock to the boil and season with nutmeg, salt and pepper. Tip the ravioli into the stock and cook for approximately 2 to 5 minutes, depending on the thickness of the ravioli. They will float when cooked. Stir the cream into the soup just before serving and sprinkle with the tarragon. Serve hot.

GLASS NOODLE SOUP

Don't worry about the name of this soup! The glass noodles are cellophane noodles and the soup also contains tasty chicken meatballs.

Serves 4

INGREDIENTS
2 tbsps oil
2 cloves garlic, thinly sliced
60g/2oz dried cellophane noodles
225g/8oz skinned and boned chicken breast
2 tbsps green curry paste
2 tbsps fish sauce
3 tbsps cornflour
1 tbsp freshly chopped coriander
1 litre/1¾ pints chicken stock
225g/8oz bok choy, shredded
4 spring onions, cut into 2.5cm/1 inch pieces

Heat the oil in a small frying pan or wok and fry the garlic until golden. Remove with a slotted spoon and drain on kitchen paper.

Place the noodles in a large bowl and cover with hot water, allow to soak until softened, then drain.

Dice the chicken, place in a food processor with the curry paste, fish sauce, cornflour and coriander, and process until very finely minced. Remove the mixture from the processor and shape into small balls. Heat the stock in a large saucepan until boiling and add the meatballs. Cook for 10-15 minutes, or until they rise to the surface. Add the softened noodles, bok choy and spring onions and continue cooking for 5 minutes. Serve garnished with the fried garlic slices.

THAI BEEF SOUP

This soup recipe uses egg noodles, but you could ring the changes by using cellophane or rice noodles. This delicious Thai recipe is an excellent dinner party soup.

Serves 4

INGREDIENTS
2 tbsps oil
225g/8oz sirloin steak, cut into thin strips
1 small onion, chopped
2 sticks celery, sliced diagonally
1.4 litres/2½ pints beef stock
1 tbsp freshly chopped coriander
2 kaffir lime leaves
2.5cm/1 inch piece fresh root ginger, peeled and thinly sliced
1 tsp palm sugar
1 tbsp fish sauce
90g/3oz egg noodles
120g/4oz canned straw mushrooms (drained weight)

Heat the oil in a wok or saucepan and fry the meat, onion and celery until the meat is cooked through and the vegetables are soft. Add the stock, coriander, lime leaves, ginger, sugar and fish sauce. Bring to the boil, then add the noodles and straw mushrooms and cook for 10 minutes. Serve piping hot.

MEATBALL SOUP

A satisfying soup for a cold winter's day. I prefer to cook the meatballs separately in the oven as they keep a better shape and texture than if they are boiled.

Serves 4

INGREDIENTS
460g/1lb beef bones
1 carrot, chopped
1 onion, chopped
1 stick celery, chopped
1 egg, beaten
225g/8oz minced beef
60g/2oz breadcrumbs
Salt and freshly ground black
  pepper
1 tbsp oil
425g/15oz can plum tomatoes
175g/6oz small pasta shapes for
  soup
1 tbsp freshly chopped parsley

Preheat the oven to 180°C/375°F/Gas Mark 4. Place the bones, carrot, onion and celery in a large saucepan and cover with cold water. Bring to the boil then cover and simmer for 1½ hours. Meanwhile, mix together the lightly beaten egg, minced beef, breadcrumbs and plenty of seasoning. Roll the mixture into small balls about the size of walnuts and place in a roasting tin with the oil. Bake in the preheated oven for 45 minutes, turning occasionally.

Strain the stock into a saucepan. Press the tomatoes and their juice through a sieve, and add to stock. Bring to the boil, and simmer for 15 minutes. Add the pasta to the stock and cook for 10 minutes, stirring frequently. Add the meatballs, adjust the seasoning, and stir in the chopped parsley. Serve hot.

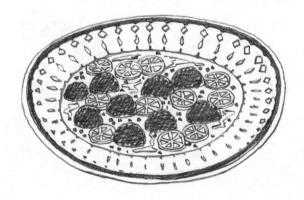

PASTA WITH VEGETABLES

Although many of the great classic pasta dishes feature meat or fish in a sauce, I find that vegetables make a perfect partnership with pasta. Providing that you have the ingredients to make fresh pasta or a packet of dried in the larder, some fresh vegetables and butter or olive oil, you have the basis of a sustaining, tasty and nutritious meal.

Pasta in the Vegetarian Diet

Pasta plays a valuable part in the diet of many vegetarians. If they eat eggs vegetarians will enjoy fresh pasta but, if not, the dried varieties do not contain egg and are therefore suitable for the stricter vegetarian diets. There are many recipes creating complicated meatless variations on the classic favourites of Bolognese sauce, lasagne and stuffed cannelloni, and they are delicious, relying on nuts, fresh herbs and vegetables such as spinach for their rich flavours. However, one vegetable fried until soft in butter or olive oil with a little garlic, and then mixed into freshly cooked pasta with plenty of black pepper and Parmesan cheese produces a sumptuous but simple meal. My favourite vegetable for cooking in this way is courgettes, and the recipe for Courgetti Spaghetti is a firm favourite in our house, especially in the late summer when courgettes are plentiful in the garden.

Pasta & Tomatoes – an Established Double Act

As Italy both produces and consumes vast quantities of tomatoes and pasta it is inevitable that tomato sauces have become one of the most popular accompaniments for pasta. I wonder just how many different recipes there are for tomato sauce? I think that an essential ingredient is fresh basil, a herb that just seems to have been invented to flavour tomatoes, but I also like to add eggs and freshly grated Parmesan if the dish of pasta and tomato sauce is to be the main meal of the day. When adding basil to sauces I find that a better flavour is obtained if the leaves are torn and not chopped – basil bruises easily and the flavour can become musty. The recipe for Tagliatelle with Rich Tomato Sauce is one of my favourites.

Pasta & Mushrooms – Dried or Fresh

Made into a sauce or served sliced, mushrooms are also an excellent choice to serve with pasta. Dried mushrooms, especially the Italian porcini, give a very strong flavour and make an excellent seasoning for any pasta dish, but I actually like to use a mixture of dried and fresh mushrooms for most dishes – I almost find dried mushrooms too overwhelming by themselves. Many people soak dried mushrooms in boiling water but I like to soak them in sherry and then to use it as part of the sauce – I use a medium sherry and it certainly adds an extra dimension to most mushroom dishes! However, you will need to leave the mushrooms to soak for at least an hour – soaking in boiling water gives much quicker results, but I prefer the slower flavour!

Pasta & Vegetable Salads

Cold cooked pasta and crisp vegetables make excellent salads, to serve either as main courses or as part of a buffet. There are many ideas for pasta salads in this chapter and they can be sophisticated dishes or hearty, family fare. I particularly like the green pasta salad with avocados, either as a supper dish or as a starter when entertaining. Pasta salads can be made more filling by adding cheese, but I often do this in the form of a cheese dressing, which gives a better, all-round blend of flavours. A blue cheese dressing on a pasta and avocado salad is high on my list of heavenly dishes!

Chinese Noodles & Seasonings

The Chinese who, like the Italians, are also great pasta eaters, often make fragrant dishes of thin egg noodles, served in a gravy-like sauce richly flavoured with such fragrant ingredients as fresh root ginger and sesame oil. If a number of vegetables are braised slowly in the sauce and freshly cooked noodles are mixed in just before serving, you have a splendid dish which simply requires an accompaniment of crispy stir-fried vegetables to be served with it. The recipe for Five Coloured Noodles is an excellent Chinese recipe for noodles and vegetables and, incidentally, it's the vegetable garnish and not the noodles themselves that are five coloured!

Just a few vegetables and a packet of pasta form the basic ingredients for so many dishes – the following is but a small selection of recipes and you will be able to create many more of your own.

STUFFED TOMATOES

*Use large, beefsteak tomatoes for this recipe – it is an ideal
starter.*

Serves 4

INGREDIENTS

4 large ripe tomatoes
460g/1lb fresh spinach
60g/2oz small pasta shapes for
  soup
30g/1oz butter, softened
1 tbsp double cream
¼ tsp grated nutmeg
1 clove garlic, crushed
Salt and freshly ground black
  pepper
1 tbsp Parmesan or Cheddar
  cheese, grated
4 anchovy fillets, halved
  lengthways

Preheat the oven to
200°C/400°F/Gas Mark 6. Cut the
tops off the tomatoes and
carefully scoop out the insides
with a teaspoon. Wash the
spinach well and remove the
stalks. Cook the spinach gently in
a large saucepan, without added
water, until it is soft. Chop the
spinach very finely or purée in a
liquidiser or food processor.
Squeeze to remove excess
moisture.

Meanwhile, cook the pasta in
boiling water for 5 minutes, or
until 'al dente'. Rinse and drain
well, then mix with the spinach.
Add the butter, cream, nutmeg
and garlic, and season well. Fill
each tomato and top with the
cheese and anchovies. Bake in
the oven for 10 minutes. Serve
immediately.

STUFFED COURGETTES

Stuffed courgettes make an elegant starter – be certain to choose evenly sized courgettes for this dish.

Serves 4

INGREDIENTS

60g/2oz small pasta shapes for soup
4 courgettes
30g/1oz butter or margarine
2 cloves garlic, crushed
1 small onion, chopped
120g/4oz minced beef
1 tsp tomato purée
Salt and freshly ground black pepper
2 tomatoes, peeled, chopped and seeds removed
60g/2oz fontina cheese, grated
1 tbsp fresh breadcrumbs

Cook the pasta in plenty of boiling, salted water for 5 minutes or until tender. Rinse in cold water and drain well. Meanwhile, place the courgettes in a pan and cover with cold water. Bring to the boil and cook gently for 3 minutes. Rinse under cold water. Cut the courgettes in half lengthways, and carefully scoop out the pulp, leaving a 1.25cm/½-inch shell. Chop the pulp.

Heat the butter in a frying pan. Add the garlic and onion and fry gently until transparent. Increase the heat and add the minced beef. Fry for 5 minutes, stirring frequently, until the meat is well browned. Stir in the tomato purée and salt and pepper to taste. Add the courgette pulp, tomatoes and pasta, and cook for 2 minutes. Spoon the mixture into the courgette shells and top with grated cheese and breadcrumbs. Brown under a grill or in a hot oven. Serve immediately.

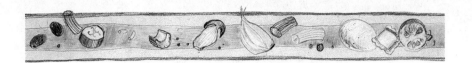

STUFFED AUBERGINES

Aubergines are very under-rated in my opinion. Baking brings out their sweet flavour.

Serves 4

INGREDIENTS
60g/2oz macaroni
4 small or 2 large aubergines
30g/1oz butter
1 small onion, chopped
1 clove garlic, crushed
225g/8oz bacon, rinded and
  diced
1 green pepper, seeded and
  diced
1 yellow pepper, seeded and
  diced
2 tomatoes, peeled, chopped and
  seeds removed
1 tbsp tomato purée
½ tsp chilli powder
Salt and freshly ground black
  pepper
60g/2oz Mozzarella cheese,
  grated
1 tbsp fresh breadcrumbs

Preheat the oven to
190°C/375°F/Gas Mark 5. Cook
the macaroni in plenty of boiling,
salted water for 10 minutes, or
until tender but still firm. Rinse in
cold water, and drain well. Wrap
the aubergines in foil and bake
in the preheated oven for 30
minutes. Cut the aubergines in
half lengthways. Scoop out the
pulp, leaving a 1.25cm/½ inch
shell, and chop the pulp.

Heat the butter in a pan. Add the
onion and garlic and cook until
soft and transparent. Add the
bacon and peppers and fry for 5
minutes, then add the aubergine
pulp, tomatoes, tomato purée,
chilli powder, and salt and
pepper. Cook for a further 3
minutes. Stir in the macaroni, and
fill the scooped-out aubergine
halves with the mixture. Top
with grated cheese and
breadcrumbs and brown under a
preheated grill or in the hot oven
at 200°C/400°F/Gas Mark 6. Serve
immediately.

COURGETTE AND PINE NUT LASAGNE WITH AUBERGINE SAUCE

Not all lasagnes are made with a meat sauce – this delicious variation is light and fragrant. It is a perfect vegetarian dinner party dish.

Serves 4

INGREDIENTS

12 sheets of wholewheat lasagne
90g/3oz pine nuts
30g/1oz butter
680g/1½lbs courgettes, trimmed and sliced
280g/10oz ricotta cheese
½ tsp nutmeg
1 tbsp olive oil
1 large aubergine, sliced
150ml/¼ pint water
Salt and freshly ground black pepper
90g/3oz Cheddar cheese, grated

Preheat the oven to 190°C/375°F/Gas Mark 5. Cook the lasagne in plenty of boiling, salted water for 8-10 minutes, then drain and leave on clean tea-towels until required. Place the pine nuts in a dry pan and roast gently over a low heat for 2 minutes. Set to one side. Melt the butter and cook the courgettes, with a little water if necessary, until just tender. Combine the courgettes, pine nuts and ricotta cheese, then add the nutmeg and mix thoroughly.

Heat the olive oil in a separate pan and cook the aubergine for 4 minutes. Add the water and simmer, covered, until soft. Season with salt and pepper. Blend in a liquidiser or food processor until smooth, adding a little extra water if necessary. Place 4 sheets of lasagne in the bottom of a greased, ovenproof dish and top with half the courgette mixture. Place 4 strips of lasagne over the courgettes and add half the aubergine sauce followed by the remaining courgettes. Cover with the remaining lasagne and the rest of the sauce. Top with the grated cheese and bake for 40 minutes, until the cheese is golden brown.

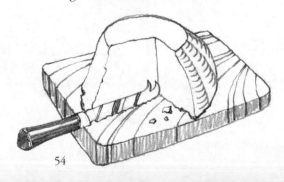

54

PASTA WITH BASIL AND TOMATO SAUCE

Use fully ripened tomatoes for this recipe, otherwise the sauce will be bland. If your fresh tomatoes are very green you will achieve better results with canned tomatoes.

Serves 4

INGREDIENTS
460g/1lb pasta, any shape
3 tbsps olive oil
1 clove garlic, chopped
3 tomatoes, peeled, seeded and
  chopped
Salt and freshly ground black
  pepper
10 fresh basil leaves, finely
  chopped

Cook the pasta in plenty of boiling, salted water. Rinse under hot water and set aside to drain. Heat the olive oil in a frying pan and cook the garlic and tomato with a little salt and pepper over a gentle heat for approximately 12 minutes, stirring frequently. Stir the well drained pasta into the sauce, mix well and heat through. Just before serving stir in the finely chopped basil, check and adjust the seasoning and serve hot.

PASTA SHELLS WITH MUSHROOM SAUCE

This tasty mushroom sauce poured over pasta makes a perfect supper dish. I sometimes add a pinch of ground mace to the sauce – add it to the mushrooms whilst they are cooking.

Serves 4

INGREDIENTS
225g/8oz button mushrooms
30g/1oz butter or margarine
30g/1oz flour
570ml/1 pint milk
Salt and freshly ground black
  pepper
280g/10oz pasta shells

Rinse the mushrooms and chop them roughly. Melt the butter in a saucepan and add the mushrooms. Fry for 5 minutes, stirring occasionally. Stir in the flour and cook for 1 minute.

Draw the pan off the heat, and add the milk gradually, stirring continuously. Return to the heat and bring to the boil, then cook for 3 minutes, stirring continuously. Season with salt and pepper.

Meanwhile, cook the pasta shells in plenty of boiling, salted water for 10 minutes, or until *al dente*. Rinse in hot water and drain well. Place in a warmed serving dish, and add the mushroom sauce. Serve immediately.

COURGETTE SALAD

I think raw courgettes are nicer than cooked ones! They make a wonderful pasta salad.

Serves 4

INGREDIENTS
225g/8oz macaroni
4 tomatoes
4-5 courgettes, thinly sliced
8 stuffed green olives, sliced
6 tbsps French dressing
Salt and freshly ground black pepper

Cook the macaroni in a large pan of boiling, salted water for 10 minutes, or until tender but still firm. Rinse in cold water and drain well.

Cut a small cross in the top of each tomato and plunge them into boiling water for 30 seconds. Carefully remove the skins from the tomatoes, using a sharp knife. Chop the tomatoes roughly. Mix all the ingredients in a large bowl and chill in the refrigerator for 30 minutes before serving. Add extra salt and pepper if necessary.

MUSHROOM PASTA SALAD

Two of my favourite salads in one! Add a clove or two of crushed garlic if you wish.

Serves 4

INGREDIENTS
5 tbsps olive oil
Juice of 2 lemons
1 tbsp freshly chopped basil
1 tbsp freshly chopped parsley
Salt and freshly ground black
  pepper
225g/8oz mushrooms, finely
  sliced
225g/8oz wholewheat pasta
  shapes of your choice

Whisk together the olive oil, lemon juice, herbs and seasonings in a large bowl. Add the sliced mushrooms to the lemon dressing, stirring well to coat the mushrooms evenly. Cover the bowl and leave to marinate in a cool place for at least 1 hour.

Cook the pasta in a large pan of boiling, salted water for 10 minutes, or until just tender. Rinse the pasta in cold water and drain well. Add the pasta to the marinated mushrooms and lemon dressing, mixing well to coat the pasta evenly. Adjust the seasoning if necessary, then chill well before serving.

GIANFOTTERE SALAD

A pasta salad which celebrates summer vegetables.

Serves 4

INGREDIENTS
1 small aubergine
2 tomatoes
1 large courgette
1 red pepper
1 green pepper
1 medium onion
1 clove garlic
4 tbsps olive oil
Freshly ground sea salt and black
  pepper
460g/1lb wholewheat pasta
  spirals or bows

Cut the aubergine into 1.25cm/½-inch slices. Sprinkle with salt and leave for 30 minutes. Chop the tomatoes roughly and remove the woody cores. Cut the courgette into 1.25cm/½-inch slices, then seed the peppers, and chop them roughly. Chop the onion and crush the garlic.

Heat 3 tbsps of olive oil in a frying pan, and cook the onion gently until it is transparent but not coloured. Rinse the salt from the aubergine thoroughly under running water and pat dry with absorbent kitchen paper. Chop the aubergine roughly then stir it, with the courgette, peppers, tomatoes and garlic, into the onion and fry gently for 20 minutes. Season with salt and pepper to taste, and allow to cool completely.

Cook the pasta spirals in plenty of boiling, salted water for 10-15 minutes, or until tender. Rinse in cold water and drain well. Place the pasta spirals in a large bowl, and stir in the remaining 1 tbsp of olive oil. Stir the vegetables into the pasta and season if necessary. Chill before serving.

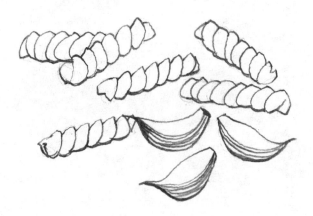

TORTIGLIONI ALLA PUTTANESCA

This is a well-flavoured sauce, typical of many areas of central and southern Italy where strongly flavoured ingredients such as chilli, anchovies and garlic are popular.

Serves 4

INGREDIENTS
200g/7oz can plum tomatoes, drained
60g/2oz can anchovy fillets, drained
280g/10oz tortiglioni, pasta spirals
2 tbsps olive oil
Pinch of chilli powder
1 clove garlic, crushed
4-5 fresh basil leaves, torn or chopped
2 tbsps freshly chopped parsley
120g/4oz black olives, pitted and chopped
Salt and freshly ground black pepper

Chop the tomatoes and remove the seeds, and chop the anchovies. Cook the pasta in plenty of boiling salted water for 10 minutes, or until tender but still firm. Rinse in hot water, drain well and place in a warmed serving dish.

Meanwhile, heat the oil in a pan, add the garlic and chilli powder and cook for 1 minute. Add the tomatoes, basil, parsley, olives and anchovies, and cook for a few minutes. Season with salt and pepper. Pour the sauce over the pasta and mix together thoroughly. Serve immediately.

FRESH PASTA WITH CEPS

A wonderful recipe of intense flavour. Buy your ceps from a reliable mushroom man if you are unsure about gathering them yourself. Alternatively, use a mixture of fresh mushrooms if ceps are not available.

Serves 4

INGREDIENTS
460g/1lb fresh pasta
200g/7oz ceps
90g/3oz butter
1-2 cloves garlic, chopped
Salt and freshly ground black
  pepper
1 tbsp freshly chopped chives

Cook the pasta in boiling, salted water, until tender. Drain, rinse and set aside to drain. Cut off the stem ends from the ceps. Wash the mushrooms carefully and dry them well, then cut into very thin slices. Heat one third of the butter and sauté the ceps with the garlic for 2 minutes. Season with plenty of salt and pepper. Add the remaining butter to the pan. When it has melted add the pasta, stir briskly, then add the chives. Cook until the pasta is heated through completely, and serve on warmed plates.

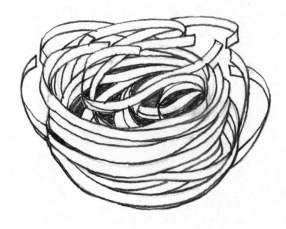

FETTUCINE ESCARGOTS WITH LEEKS AND SUN-DRIED TOMATOES

Canned snails are delicious in dishes such as this, where they are flavoured with garlic, mushrooms and dried tomatoes.

Serves 4-6

INGREDIENTS

6 sun-dried tomatoes
400g/14oz can escargots (snails), drained
340g/12oz fresh or dried whole-wheat fettucine (tagliatelle)
3 tbsps olive oil
2 cloves garlic, crushed
1 large or 2 small leeks, trimmed and finely sliced
6 oyster, shiitake or other large mushrooms, sliced
4 tbsps chicken or vegetable stock
3 tbsps dry white wine
6 tbsps double cream
1 tbsp freshly chopped basil
1 tbsp freshly chopped parsley
Salt and freshly ground black pepper

Chop the sun-dried tomatoes roughly. Drain the escargots well and dry on absorbent kitchen paper.

Place the fettucine in boiling, salted water and cook for about 10-12 minutes, or until *al dente*. Drain, rinse under hot water and leave in a colander to drain again. Meanwhile, heat the olive oil in a frying pan and add the garlic and leeks. Cook slowly until just starting to soften then add the mushrooms and cook until the leeks are just slightly crisp. Remove the vegetables to a plate. Add the drained escargots to the pan and cook over a high heat for about 2 minutes, stirring constantly. Add the stock and wine and bring to the boil. Boil to reduce by about a quarter, then add the cream and the chopped sun-dried tomatoes. Bring to the boil then cook slowly for about 3 minutes. Add the herbs and salt and pepper to taste. Add the leeks, mushrooms and fettucine to the pan and heat through. Serve immediately.

PASTA PAPRIKA

This is pasta served in the style of a goulash, with plenty of peppers, tomato and paprika for seasoning.

Serves 4

INGREDIENTS

340g/12oz green or wholewheat
  fettucine, fresh or dried
1 tsp sunflower oil
1 tbsp olive oil
1 large onion, chopped
1 clove garlic, crushed
2 tsps paprika
3 small peppers, one green, one
  red and one yellow, seeded
  and sliced
460g/1lb passata
Salt and freshly ground black
  pepper
60g/2oz Parmesan cheese

Place the pasta in a large pan of boiling, salted water and add the sunflower oil. Cook for 8-15 minutes until the pasta is tender. Dried pasta will take longer to cook than fresh. Drain the cooked pasta while preparing the sauce.

Heat the olive oil and fry the onion, garlic, paprika and sliced peppers for about 8 minutes until softened. Add the passata and mix well. Add the vegetables and sauce mixture to the pasta and stir well, then season to taste. Return the mixture to a large saucepan and heat through gently for 5 minutes. Serve immediately, topped with Parmesan cheese.

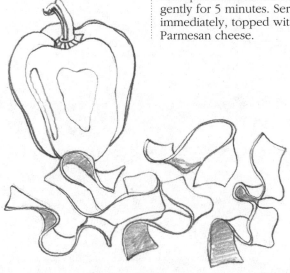

FARFALLE WITH TOMATO SAUCE

Tomato sauce is a favourite with any type of pasta.

Serves 2

INGREDIENTS
1 tbsp olive oil
2 cloves garlic, crushed
1 onion, sliced
1 tbsp fresh basil leaves, roughly torn
2 400g/14oz cans plum tomatoes, chopped
Salt and freshly ground black pepper
280g/10oz farfalle (pasta bows)
2 tbsps freshly chopped basil or parsley
Parmesan cheese, grated

Heat the oil in a deep pan, add the garlic and onion, and cook until softened. Add the torn basil, and cook for 30 seconds, then add the undrained tomatoes and season with salt and pepper. Bring to the boil, reduce the heat and simmer, uncovered, for about 20 minutes, or until the sauce is reduced by half.

Meanwhile, cook the pasta in a large pan of boiling, salted water until tender but still firm – about 10 minutes. Rinse in hot water, and drain well. Press the sauce through a sieve, and stir in the fresh parsley or basil. Toss the sauce through the pasta. Serve immediately with grated Parmesan cheese.

SPINACH LASAGNE

Easy-cook lasagne is available, but it doesn't taste as good or cook as tender as that which you boil before baking.

Serves 4

INGREDIENTS
8 sheets green lasagne

Spinach sauce
60g/2oz butter or margarine
60g/2oz flour
280ml/½ pint milk
300g/11oz frozen spinach,
  thawed and finely chopped
Pinch of ground nutmeg
Salt and freshly ground black
  pepper

Mornay sauce
30g/1oz butter or margarine
30g/1oz flour
280ml/½ pint milk
90g/3oz Parmesan cheese, grated
1 tsp French mustard
Salt

To make the spinach sauce, heat the butter in a pan, stir in the flour and cook for 30 seconds. Draw the pan off the heat, and gradually stir in the milk. Return to the heat and bring to the boil, stirring continuously. Cook for 3 minutes, then add the spinach, nutmeg, and salt and pepper to taste. Set aside until needed.

Preheat the oven to 200°C/400°F/Gas Mark 6. Cook the spinach lasagne in plenty of boiling, salted water for 10 minutes, or until tender. Rinse in cold water, and drain carefully. Dry on a clean cloth. To make the mornay sauce, heat the butter in a pan and stir in the flour, cooking for 30 seconds. Remove from the heat, and stir in the milk. Return to the heat, stirring continuously, until boiling. Continue stirring, and simmer for 3 minutes. Add the mustard, two-thirds of cheese, and salt to taste, then leave until required.

Grease an ovenproof baking dish. Line the base with a layer of lasagne, followed by some of the spinach mixture, and a layer of cheese sauce. Repeat the process, finishing with a layer of lasagne and a covering of the cheese sauce. Scatter the remaining cheese over the lasagne. Bake in the hot oven until golden, about 20-30 minutes. Serve immediately.

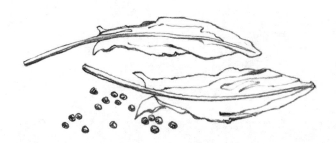

CANNELLONI WITH TOMATO AND CHEESE

A filling of cheese and tomato, flavoured with basil, makes this a popular dish with vegetarians and meat-eaters alike.

Serves 4

INGREDIENTS
12 cannelloni shells

Filling
400g/14oz can plum tomatoes
120g/4oz ricotta cheese
1 tsp tomato purée
1 tbsp freshly chopped basil
120g/4oz Parmesan cheese, grated
Salt and freshly ground black pepper

Sauce
1 tbsp olive oil
1 onion, chopped
400g/14oz can plum tomatoes
1 tbsp cornflour
Salt and freshly ground black pepper
30g/1oz Parmesan cheese, grated

Cook the cannelloni shells in a large pan of boiling salted water for 15-20 minutes, until tender. Rinse in hot water and drain well.

Chop the tomatoes for the filling and remove the pips. Set the juice aside for the sauce. Beat the ricotta cheese until smooth, then add the tomato purée, basil and Parmesan cheese and beat well. Stir in the chopped tomato and salt and pepper to taste. Fill the cannelloni shells with a teaspoon or a piping bag with a wide, plain nozzle. Place in a greased ovenproof dish.

Heat the oil for the sauce in a pan and cook the onion gently until transparent. Push the tomatoes and their juice through a sieve into the saucepan. Mix the cornflour with the reserved tomato juice and add it to the pan. Bring to the boil and cook for 3 minutes, stirring continuously. Add salt and pepper to taste. Pour the sauce over the cannelloni and sprinkle with the cheese. Place under a preheated grill for 10 minutes, until heated through. Serve immediately.

PASTA WITH TOMATO AND YOGURT SAUCE

I wonder how many recipes there are for tomato sauce? Serve this dish with the yogurt topping the sauce, or marbled through the tomato mixture just before it is added to the pasta.

Serves 4

INGREDIENTS
15g/½oz butter or margarine
15g/½oz flour
150ml/¼ pint beef stock
400g/14oz can plum tomatoes
1 bay leaf
Sprig of thyme
Parsley stalks
280g/10oz pasta shells
Salt and freshly ground black
  pepper
3 tbsps natural yogurt

Melt the butter in a pan. Stir in the flour and cook for about 1 minute, then add the stock gradually. Add the undrained tomatoes, bay leaf, thyme and parsley stalks and season with salt and pepper. Bring to the boil, stirring all the time, then simmer for 30 minutes. Press the sauce through a sieve back into a clean pan, adjust the seasoning, and reheat.

Meanwhile, cook the pasta in plenty of boiling salted water for 10 minutes, or until tender but still firm. Rinse in hot water and drain well. Place in a warmed serving dish and pour the tomato sauce over. Top with the yogurt. Serve immediately.

PASTA SPIRALS WITH PEAS AND TOMATOES

Peas are widely used in Italian cookery – they provide colour and texture in this dish.

Serves 4

INGREDIENTS
280g/10oz pasta spirals
340g/12oz shelled peas
1 tsp sugar
60g/2oz butter or margarine
1 tbsp freshly chopped basil
400g/14oz can chopped tomatoes
Salt and freshly ground black
   pepper

Cook the pasta spirals in plenty of boiling, salted water for 10 minutes or until tender. Drain. Meanwhile, cook the peas in boiling water with a pinch of salt and a teaspoon of sugar. Melt the butter in a pan, add the basil and cook for 30 seconds. Add the tomatoes and their juice. When hot, add the pasta spirals, peas and salt and pepper to taste. Toss together and serve immediately.

SPAGHETTI NEAPOLITANA

This is one of the classic tomato sauces – simple but packed with flavour.

Serves 4

INGREDIENTS
2 400g/14oz cans plum tomatoes
2 tbsps olive oil
1 tbsp freshly chopped oregano
   or marjoram
Salt and freshly ground black
   pepper
280g/10oz spaghetti
2 tbsps freshly chopped parsley
Parmesan cheese, grated

Press the undrained tomatoes through a sieve. Heat the oil in a pan, add the oregano or marjoram and cook for 30 seconds. Add the puréed tomatoes, and salt and pepper and bring to the boil. Reduce the heat and simmer, uncovered, for 20-30 minutes.

Meanwhile, cook the spaghetti in plenty of boiling, salted water for about 10 minutes, or until tender but still firm. Rinse under hot water, and drain well. Pour the tomato sauce over the spaghetti, and toss gently. Sprinkle with the parsley and serve with the Parmesan cheese.

SPINACH RAVIOLI

Spinach makes an unusual but tasty filling for this dish of ravioli.

Serves 4

INGREDIENTS

Dough
250g/9oz strong plain flour
3 eggs, lightly beaten

Filling
225g/8oz cooked spinach
30g/1oz butter or margarine
60g/2oz Parmesan cheese, grated
Pinch of grated nutmeg
Salt and freshly ground black
  pepper
1 egg, beaten

Cheese Sauce
30g/1oz butter or margarine
15g/½oz flour
280ml/½ pint milk
1 tsp French mustard
30g/1oz Parmesan cheese, grated

Prepare the filling. Chop the spinach and heat it in a pan, then beat in the butter. Add the Parmesan cheese, nutmeg and salt and freshly ground black pepper to taste. Finally mix in the beaten egg. Set aside until required.

Prepare the dough by sifting the flour into a bowl; make a well in the centre and add the eggs. Work the flour and the eggs together with a spoon, and then knead by hand until a smooth dough is formed. Leave to rest for 15 minutes. Lightly flour a work surface and roll out the dough thinly into a rectangle. Cut the dough in half. Shape the filling into small balls and set them about 4cm/1½-inches apart on one half of the dough. Place the other half on top, and cut with a ravioli cutter or small pastry cutter. Seal the edges. Cook in batches in a large pan with plenty of boiling, salted water until tender – about 8 minutes. Remove the ravioli carefully with a slotted spoon. Meanwhile, make the sauce.

Heat the butter in a pan. Add the flour and cook for 30 seconds. Draw the pan off the heat, and gradually add the milk. Bring to the boil and simmer for 3 minutes, stirring continuously. Add the mustard and half the cheese, and seasoning to taste. Pour the sauce over the ravioli and serve immediately with the remaining cheese sprinkled over the top.

SPINACH-STUFFED CANNELLONI

Mozzarella, spinach and ham is one of my favourite pizza toppings – it is also a delicious filling for cannelloni.

Serves 4

INGREDIENTS
12 cannelloni shells
60g/2oz butter
225g/8oz spinach, washed and
   finely shredded
3 slices ham, cut into thin strips
225g/8oz mozzarella cheese, cut
   into small cubes
30g/1oz flour
280ml/½ pint milk
Pinch of nutmeg
Salt and freshly ground black
   pepper
45g/1½oz Parmesan cheese,
   grated

Preheat the oven to
200°C/400°F/Gas Mark 6. Cook
the cannelloni in boiling, salted
water, removing them when they
are still quite firm (approximately
5 minutes). Rinse them in hot
water and set aside to drain on a
slightly damp tea-towel.

Heat half the butter in a frying
pan and gently cook the spinach
and the ham for 2 minutes.
Remove from the heat and stir in
the mozzarella cheese. Fill each
of the cannelloni with the
mixture and place them in a
greased ovenproof dish. Melt the
remaining butter in a pan and stir
in the flour. Cook for about 1
minute then draw the pan off the
heat and gradually stir in the
milk. Bring to the boil, stirring
continuously, then cook for 2-3
minutes. Season to taste with
nutmeg, salt and pepper. Pour
the sauce over the filled
cannelloni and top with
Parmesan cheese. Cook in the
hot oven for 15 minutes. Serve
piping hot.

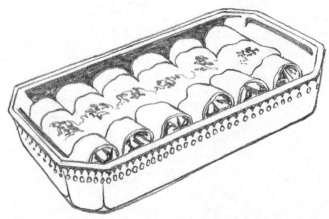

SPINACH TAGLIATELLE WITH CREAM SAUCE

I sometimes add a little freshly grated nutmeg to this sauce. The dish is a simple celebration of fragrant flavours.

Serves 4

INGREDIENTS
300g/11oz flour
2 eggs
120g/4oz spinach, cooked and chopped
2 tbsps freshly chopped chives
200ml/7fl oz single cream
Salt and freshly ground black pepper

Mix together the flour, eggs and spinach in a large bowl. Mix well and form the dough into a ball. Knead lightly then sprinkle the dough with flour and set aside in the refrigerator for 30 minutes. Roll out the dough with a rolling pin or pass it through the rollers of a pasta machine and then cut it into tagliatelle. Spread the strips out on a floured surface; the strips should not touch one another. Allow to dry for a few minutes.

Bring a large pan of salted water to the boil, add the pasta and cook until *al dente*. Rinse under hot water and set aside to drain. Heat together the chives and cream, add the pasta to the pan, stir well and serve when the pasta is heated through. Season with a little salt and pepper if necessary.

TAGLIATELLE WITH SAUTÉED VEGETABLES

A delicious recipe for fresh pasta with summer vegetables

Serves 4

INGREDIENTS
300g/11oz flour
2 eggs, beaten
2 tbsps olive oil
1 red pepper, seeded and cut
 into thin strips
2 courgettes, thickly peeled
 (keep the peel and discard the
 rest)
Salt and freshly ground black
 pepper
60g/2oz butter

Make the dough by mixing together the flour and eggs. Work the dough with your fingertips and form into a ball. Set aside to rest in the refrigerator for 30 minutes, wrapped. Pass the dough through the rollers of a pasta machine, flouring the dough lightly to prevent sticking. Alternatively, roll out the dough with a rolling pin. Pass the strips through the pasta machine fitted with a tagliatelle cutter, or cut into strips with a sharp knife. Spread the tagliatelle out on a tea-towel and leave to dry for 30 minutes.

Heat the olive oil in a frying pan and sauté the pepper for 2 minutes, stirring frequently. Add strips of the courgette peel and continue cooking for 45 seconds. Pour off the excess fat and season with salt and pepper. Keep warm. Cook the tagliatelle in boiling, salted water for about 3 minutes, then rinse under hot water and set to drain. Set the frying pan containing the vegetables over the heat, stir in the butter and then stir in the tagliatelle. Heat thoroughly and serve immediately.

NOODLE VEGETABLE RING

An unusual way of serving tagliatelle. Pack the noodles firmly into the mould, so that they will release easily for serving.

Serves 4-6

INGREDIENTS
90g/3oz egg noodles or thin
  tagliatelle
Oil
45g/1½oz butter or margarine
3 tbsps flour
340ml/12fl oz milk
Salt, freshly ground black pepper
  and paprika
225g/8oz Cheddar cheese, grated
2 eggs, beaten
60g/2oz mixed peas and carrots,
  cooked
120g/4oz broccoli florets, cooked
60g/2oz sweetcorn, cooked
1 small red pepper, seeded and
  diced

Preheat the oven to 180°C/350°F/Gas Mark 4. Cook the egg noodles in boiling, salted water until just tender. Drain well and toss with a little oil to prevent them from sticking.

Melt the butter or margarine in a saucepan, then stir in the flour. Cook for about 1 minute, then gradually beat in the milk until smooth. Add a good pinch of salt, pepper and paprika. Bring the sauce to the boil, stirring continuously, and cook until thick. Add the cheese and stir until melted. Divide the sauce in two.

Add half the sauce and the eggs to the noodles and mix thoroughly. Spoon the mixture into a well-greased ring mould. Place the mould in a roasting tin containing enough hot water to come halfway up the sides of the mould. Bake in the preheated oven for about 45 minutes, or until completely set.

Meanwhile, combine the cooked vegetables with the diced pepper and the remaining cheese sauce. If the sauce is too thick, add a little more milk. Unmould the noodle ring on to a large platter and sprinkle with paprika. Spoon the vegetables in their sauce into the middle and serve.

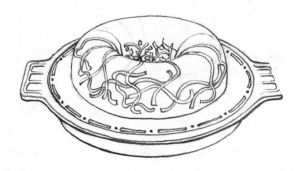

TAGLIATELLE WITH DRIED MUSHROOMS AND CREAM

*Dried mushrooms have a very intense flavour. I like to make
this dish with a mixture of dried and fresh mushrooms.*

Serves 4-6

INGREDIENTS
45g/1½oz dried mushrooms or
   225g/8oz fresh
3 tbsp olive oil
1 medium onion, chopped
460g/1lb tagliatelle
120ml/4fl oz single cream
30g/1oz Parmesan cheese, grated
2 tbsp freshly chopped parsley
Salt and freshly ground black
   pepper

Soak the dried mushrooms in
water for 2-3 hours. Drain and
squeeze out the liquid, then
chop the mushrooms roughly.
Heat the oil in a small pan and
sauté the chopped onion for 1-2
minutes. Add the mushrooms
and cook for a further 10
minutes. Meanwhile, cook the
tagliatelle in plenty of boiling,
salted water. Drain and return
the pasta to the pan. Stir in the
mushrooms, cream, cheese and
parsley. Season well with salt
and pepper. Stir until heated
through and well mixed. Serve at
once.

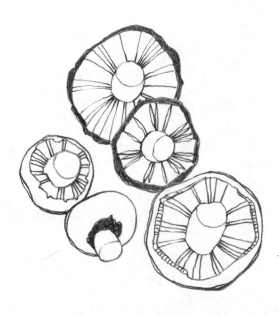

CHINESE NOODLES WITH VEGETABLES

This pasta dish has a taste of the Orient about it. Add fresh mushrooms to the other vegetables in the frying pan if Chinese dried mushrooms are not available.

Serves 4

INGREDIENTS
2 tbsps dried black Chinese mushrooms
2 carrots
¼ cucumber
200g/7oz can bamboo shoots
30g/1oz bean sprouts
400g/14oz Chinese noodles
3 tbsps oil
3 slices fresh root ginger, peeled
1 clove garlic, finely chopped
1 small chilli, finely chopped
5 tbsps soy sauce
1 tbsp honey
Salt and freshly ground black pepper
Freshly chopped chives

Soak the mushrooms for 15 minutes in boiling water. Drain, then discard the stalks and boil the mushroom caps for 5 minutes. Cut the carrots into matchsticks. Squeeze the water from the mushrooms and slice the caps. Cut the cucumber into chunks. Peel the chunks thickly and discard the seeds. Cut into matchsticks, then cut the bamboo shoots into matchsticks. Blanch the bamboo shoots for 2 minutes, then drain and set aside. Wash the bean sprouts, blanch for 1 minute, then plunge into cold water and drain.

Cook the noodles in boiling salted water for a few minutes, the exact cooking time will depend on the thickness of the noodles. Drain, rinse and set aside. Heat the oil in a frying pan and fry the ginger, garlic and chilli for a few seconds. Add the bamboo shoots, mushrooms and carrots. Fry for 4 minutes then add the bean sprouts. Cook for a further 2 minutes. Add the noodles, soy sauce and honey. Stir well and heat through. Add the cucumber at the last moment. Heat for 1 minute then season to taste with salt and pepper. Garnish with the chives and serve.

FIVE-COLOURED NOODLES

It's not the pasta which is five-coloured, it's the vegetables that are served with it!

Serves 4

INGREDIENTS

4 dried shiitake mushrooms, soaked for 30 minutes, drained and stalks removed, sliced
225g/8oz Chinese noodles or thin tagliatelle
150ml/¼ pint chicken stock
1 carrot, cut into diagonal slices
1 small turnip, diced
120g/4oz French beans, cut into 4cm/1½ inch slices
2 tsps cornflour
3 tbsps light soy sauce
4 tsps black sesame seeds

Prepare the dried mushrooms. Cook the noodles in plenty of boiling, salted water for 5 minutes. Drain and rinse under cold water then drain thoroughly. Bring the stock to the boil in a separate pan, add the carrot, turnip, mushrooms and beans, cover and simmer for 8-10 minutes, until just tender. Blend the cornflour and soy sauce together and add to the stock. Continue cooking until slightly thickened. Divide the noodles among 4 serving bowls and add the vegetables. Sprinkle with the black sesame seeds and serve.

BRAISED NOODLES

I love noodle dishes with plenty of spicy flavours and rich gravy. A large napkin will protect your clothing while you enjoy this dish!

Serves 4

INGREDIENTS
225g/8oz Chinese noodles
3 tbsps oil
6 spring onions, chopped
1 small piece fresh root ginger, grated
280ml/½ pint chicken or vegetable stock
2 tbsps soy sauce

Garnish
2 red chillies, seeded and finely chopped
2 tbsps freshly chopped coriander
60g/2oz chopped roasted peanuts

Cook the noodles in boiling, salted water until just tender. Drain them and rinse under hot water. Toss in a colander to remove excess water. Heat the oil in a wok or heavy-based pan and cook the spring onions and ginger for about 1 minute. Add the noodles and fry on one side until golden brown. Turn over and fry on the other side until golden. Mix the stock and soy sauce together and gradually pour over the noodles. Simmer for about 5 minutes, stirring occasionally to help separate the noodles. Serve in individual bowls, sprinkled with the garnish.

STIR-FRIED THAI NOODLES

This is a classic Thai dish. Much of the flavour comes from the pickled turnip, which is not always easy to find, so stock up whenever you are near a speciality food shop.

Serves 4

INGREDIENTS

175g/6oz rice noodles
4 tbsps oil
225g/8oz tofu, cut into cubes
3 cloves garlic, crushed
60g/2oz dried shrimps
3 tbsps chopped pickled turnip
4 tbsps fish sauce
30g/1oz palm sugar
1 tbsp soy sauce
2 tbsps tamarind juice
2 eggs, beaten
1 tbsp freshly chopped garlic
    chives
60g/2oz roasted peanuts,
    chopped
225g/8oz bean sprouts
Chilli strips, to garnish

Soak the rice noodles in boiling water for 10-15 minutes or until softened, then drain and set aside.

Heat the oil in a wok and fry the tofu cubes until browned on all sides. Remove with a slotted spoon and set aside. Add the garlic and dried shrimps to the wok and stir-fry for 2 minutes. Reduce the heat and add the noodles. Cook for 5 minutes, tossing the ingredients frequently. Add the pickled turnip, fish sauce, sugar, soy sauce and tamarind juice and cook for 2 minutes. Add the beaten egg and cook, tossing the ingredients together until the egg sets. Stir in the tofu, garlic chives, peanuts and bean sprouts. Garnish with chilli strips and serve immediately.

PASTA AND VEGETABLES IN PARMESAN DRESSING

The only problem with this recipe is that the dressing is so delicious that I tend to eat it by itself!

Serves 6

INGREDIENTS
460g/1lb pasta spirals or other
  shapes
225g/8oz assorted vegetables
  such as:
Courgettes, cut in rounds or
  matchsticks
Broccoli, trimmed into very small
  florets
Mangetout, trimmed
Carrots, cut in rounds or
  matchsticks
Celery, cut in matchsticks
Spring onions, thinly shredded or
  sliced
Asparagus tips
French beans, sliced
Red or yellow peppers, seeded
  and thinly sliced
Cucumber, cut in matchsticks

Dressing
150ml/¼ pint olive oil
3 tbsp lemon juice
1 tbsp pepper sauce
1 tbsp freshly chopped parsley
1 tbsp freshly chopped basil
60g/2oz Parmesan cheese, grated
2 tbsps mild mustard
Salt and freshly ground black
  pepper
Pinch of sugar

Cook the pasta in a large pan of boiling salted water for 10-12 minutes or until just tender. Rinse under hot water then leave in cold water. Cook all the vegetables except the cucumber in boiling salted water for 3 minutes until just tender. Rinse in cold water and leave to drain. Mix the dressing ingredients together. Drain the pasta thoroughly and toss it with the dressing. Add the vegetables and toss until coated. Refrigerate for up to 1 hour before serving.

TAGLIATELLE WITH SUMMER SAUCE

This recipe is slightly unusual as a cold sauce is added to hot pasta – but it works well.

Serves 4

INGREDIENTS

Pasta Dough
120g/4oz plain flour
120g/4oz fine semolina
2 large eggs, lightly beaten
2 tsps olive oil

Sauce
460g/1lb unpeeled tomatoes,
  seeded and chopped
1 large green pepper, seeded and
  diced
1 onion, chopped
1 tbsp freshly chopped basil
1 tbsp freshly chopped parsley
2 cloves garlic, crushed
150ml/¼ pint olive oil and
  vegetable oil, mixed

Place the flour and semolina in a bowl and make a well in the centre. Place the eggs and oil in the well and mix to a dough, using a fork and then your hand. Knead the dough until smooth then cover the dough and leave it to rest for 15 minutes. Divide the dough into quarters and roll it out thinly with a rolling pin on a floured surface or use a pasta machine, dusting the dough lightly with flour before rolling. Allow the sheets of pasta to dry for about 10 minutes on a floured surface or tea towels. Cut the sheets into strips about 6mm/¼ inch wide by hand or machine, dusting lightly with flour while cutting. Leave the cut pasta to dry while preparing the sauce

Combine all the sauce ingredients, mixing well. The flavour will develop if the sauce can be left to marinate. Cook the pasta for 5-6 minutes in boiling, salted water. Drain the pasta and rinse under very hot water. Toss in a colander to drain excess water. Place the hot pasta in serving dish. Pour the cold sauce over and toss. Serve immediately.

SPAGHETTI AMATRICIANA

This is a dish of spaghetti with a spicy tomato sauce. Serve with grated Parmesan, if required.

Serves 4

INGREDIENTS
1 onion
6 rashers smoked back bacon
460g/1lb ripe tomatoes
1 red chilli
1½ tbsps oil
340g/12oz spaghetti

Slice the onion thinly. Remove the rind from the bacon and cut it into thin strips. Scald the tomatoes in boiling water for 6-8 seconds. Remove with a draining spoon and place in cold water, and leave to cool completely. Skin the tomatoes and cut them in half, then remove the seeds and pulp with a teaspoon. Rub the seeds and pulp through a strainer and retain the juice to use in the sauce if desired. Chop the tomato flesh roughly and set it aside. Cut the stem off the chilli and cut it in half lengthways. Remove the seeds and core and cut the chilli into thin strips. Cut the strips into small dice.

Heat the oil in a sauté or frying pan and add the onion and bacon. Stir over a medium heat for about 5 minutes, until the onion is transparent. Drain off any excess fat, add the tomatoes and chilli and mix well. Simmer the sauce gently, uncovered, for about 5 minutes, stirring occasionally. Meanwhile, cook the spaghetti in boiling, salted water for about 10-12 minutes. Drain and rinse in hot water and toss in a colander to dry. To serve, spoon the sauce on top of the spaghetti.

LASAGNE NAPOLETANA

Lasagne as eaten in Napoli – with a tomato sauce. Ideal for vegetarians.

Serves 6

INGREDIENTS
9 sheets spinach lasagne

Tomato Sauce
3 tbsps olive oil
2 cloves garlic, crushed
900g/2lbs fresh tomatoes, skinned, or canned tomatoes, drained
2 tbsps freshly chopped basil, six whole leaves reserved
Salt and freshly ground black pepper
Pinch of sugar

Cheese Filling
460g/1lb ricotta cheese
60g/2oz unsalted butter
225g/8oz mozzarella cheese, grated
Salt and freshly ground black pepper
Pinch of nutmeg

Preheat the oven to 190°C/375°F/Gas Mark 5. Cook the pasta for 8 minutes in boiling, salted water. Drain and rinse under hot water and place in a single layer on a damp tea towel until required.

To prepare the sauce, cook the garlic in the oil for about 1 minute in a large pan. When pale brown, add the tomatoes, basil, salt, pepper and sugar. If using fresh tomatoes, drop into boiling water for 6-8 seconds. Transfer to cold water and leave to cool completely before removing the skins. This will make the skins easier to remove. Simmer the sauce for 35 minutes. Add more seasoning or sugar to taste. Beat the ricotta cheese and butter for the filling together until creamy, then stir in the remaining ingredients.

To assemble the lasagne, oil a rectangular ovenproof dish and place 3 sheets of lasagne in the base. Cover with one third of the sauce and carefully add a layer of cheese. Place another 3 sheets of pasta over the cheese and cover with another third of the sauce. Add the remaining cheese filling and cover with the remaining pasta. Spoon the remaining sauce on top. Cover with foil and bake for 20 minutes in the preheated oven. Uncover and cook for a further 10 minutes. Garnish with the reserved basil leaves before serving.

SPIRALI WITH SPINACH AND BACON

A quick and tasty dish to prepare – I often add freshly grated nutmeg, the perfect partner for spinach.

Serves 4

INGREDIENTS
340g/12oz pasta spirals
225g/8oz fresh spinach
90g/3oz bacon rashers
1 small chilli, red or green
1 small red pepper
1 small onion
3 tbsps olive oil
1 clove garlic, crushed
Salt and freshly ground black
  pepper

Cook the pasta in boiling, salted water for about 10-12 minutes or until just tender. Drain in a colander and rinse under hot water. Keep the pasta in a bowl of hot water until ready to use.

Tear the stalks off the spinach and wash the leaves well, changing the water several times. Set aside to drain. Remove any rind and bones from the bacon, and dice the bacon finely. Cut the chilli and the red pepper in half, remove the seeds and slice finely. Slice the onion thinly. Roll up several of the spinach leaves into a cigar shape and then shred them finely. Repeat until all the spinach is shredded.

Heat the oil in a sauté or frying pan and add the garlic, onion, peppers and bacon. Fry for 2 minutes then add the spinach and fry for a further 2 minutes, stirring continuously. Season with salt and pepper. Drain the pasta and toss it in a colander to remove excess water. Mix with the spinach sauce and serve immediately.

NOODLES WITH GINGER AND OYSTER SAUCE

This makes a very good accompaniment to any Chinese meat or chicken dishes, but is also a tasty supper snack on its own.

Serves 4 or 2 as a supper dish

INGREDIENTS

225g/8oz Chinese noodles
1 carrot
1 courgette
3 slices of fresh ginger root, peeled
1 tbsp oil
1 spring onion, finely sliced
1 tbsp soy sauce
2 tbsps oyster sauce
Salt and freshly ground black pepper

Cook the noodles in boiling, salted water as directed, rinse them under cold water, and set aside to drain. Cut the carrot into thin strips. Thickly peel the courgette to include a little of the flesh and cut the peel into thin strips. Discard the centre of the courgette. Peel the fresh ginger root sparingly, but remove any hard parts. Cut into thin slices, using a potato peeler. Cut the slices into thin strips, using a very sharp knife. Heat the oil in a wok, and stir-fry the spring onion for 10 seconds; add the carrot, courgette and ginger, and stir-fry briefly. Stir in the noodles and cook for 1 minute. Stir in the soy and oyster sauces, and continue cooking until heated through. Season with salt and pepper and serve.

SPICY FRIED NOODLES

*This recipe may be made with thread egg noodles or the thin,
flat mie noodles, which are like fine tagliatelle. I actually
prefer to use the latter.*

Serves 4

INGREDIENTS
225g/8oz Chinese noodles
3 tbsps oil
1 medium onion, finely chopped
2 cloves garlic, crushed
1 small piece fresh root ginger,
   grated
½ tsp ground cumin
½ tsp ground coriander
¼ tsp ground nutmeg
¼ tsp ground cinnamon
¼ tsp cayenne pepper
Salt and pepper
6 tbsps soy sauce

Garnish
Thin omelette strips
1 stick celery, very thinly
   shredded

Cook the noodles in boiling,
salted water until just tender.
Drain and refresh under hot
water, tossing in a colander to
remove excess water. Heat the
oil in a large, heavy-based frying
pan or wok and fry the onion,
garlic and ginger until softened.
Add the spices and cook for a
further 2 minutes. Stir in the
noodles and then fry over a
gentle heat for about 3 minutes.
Add the soy sauce and season
with salt and pepper. Serve
topped with the garnishes.

TOFU WITH CRISPY NOODLES

Fried noodles give a wonderful crispy texture to this unusual dish.

Serves 4

INGREDIENTS

Oil for deep-frying
120g/4oz rice noodles (vermicelli)
225g/8oz tofu, drained and patted dry
2 carrots, peeled and sliced
90g/3oz broccoli florets
2 sticks celery, sliced
1 onion, cut into wedges
1 tsp shrimp paste
2 tbsps light soy sauce
3 tbsps white wine vinegar
2 tbsps dark muscovado sugar
1 tsp grated fresh root ginger

Heat the oil to 180°C/360°F in a wok. Add the rice noodles in small batches, turn over and fry for a few seconds. The noodles will puff up immediately. Remove from the oil and drain well on absorbent kitchen paper.

Cut the tofu into cubes and fry for a few minutes until browned on all sides; remove from the oil and set aside.

Pour off most of the oil, add the carrots, broccoli, celery and onion to the wok and stir-fry for 2 minutes or until the vegetables are cooked but still crisp. Stir in the shrimp paste, soy sauce, vinegar, sugar and ginger. Return the vermicelli and tofu to the wok, toss to mix, and serve immediately.

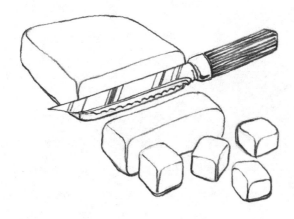

NOODLES WITH PEPPERS AND GINGER

This is a very fragrant way of cooking noodles. Cutting the peppers so finely releases plenty of flavour from the vegetables.

Serves 4

INGREDIENTS
1 red pepper, seeded
1 green pepper, seeded
225g/8oz Chinese noodles
1 tbsp oil
1 tsp chopped fresh root ginger
Salt and freshly ground black
  pepper
1 clove garlic, finely chopped

Cut the peppers into six pieces. Cut each of these pieces in half through the flesh of the pepper, to form wide, thin slices. Cut each slice into very thin matchsticks. Cook the noodles until just tender in boiling, lightly salted water, stirring occasionally so that they do not stick. Drain the noodles in a sieve and rinse under cold running water. Set aside to drain. Heat the oil in a wok and stir-fry the peppers, ginger and garlic for 1 minute, stirring continuously. Add the well-drained noodles and stir-fry until the noodles are hot. Season to taste and serve immediately.

PASTA AND ASPARAGUS SALAD

I can never decide whether green or egg pasta looks best in this elegant, summer salad.

Serves 4

INGREDIENTS

120g/4oz tagliatelle or other pasta shapes
460g/1lb asparagus, trimmed and cut into 2.5cm/1 inch pieces
2 courgettes, cut into 5cm/2 inch sticks
2 tbsps freshly chopped parsley
2 tbsps freshly chopped marjoram
1 lemon, peeled and segmented
Grated rind and juice of 1 lemon
90ml/3fl oz olive oil
Pinch of unrefined sugar
Salt and freshly ground black pepper
Crisp lettuce leaves
Frisée leaves

Cook the pasta in plenty of boiling, salted water for 10 minutes, or as directed on the packet. Drain and refresh in cold water. Drain again and leave to cool completely. Cook the asparagus in lightly salted, boiling water for 4 minutes, then add the courgettes and cook for a further 3 to 4 minutes or until the vegetables are just tender. Drain and refresh in cold water. Drain again and leave to cool.

Place the cooked pasta, vegetables, herbs and lemon segments into a large bowl, taking care not to break up the vegetables. Mix together the lemon rind, juice, oil, sugar, salt and pepper to make the dressing. Arrange the lettuce and frisée on serving plates. Just before serving, pour the dressing over the vegetables and pasta and toss to coat well. Pile equal quantities of the pasta salad into the centre of the salad leaves and serve immediately.

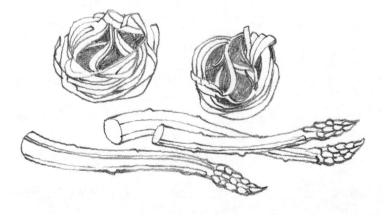

PASTA, PEAS AND PEPPERS

This colourful supper dish is also an excellent salad to serve as part of a buffet.

Serves 4

INGREDIENTS

225g/8oz mixed, plain and
  wholemeal, pasta shells
Salt
225g/8oz shelled peas
1 green pepper, seeded and
  sliced
1 red pepper, seeded and sliced
1 yellow pepper, seeded and
  sliced
150ml/¼ pint vegetable or olive
  oil
4 tbsps white wine vinegar
1 tbsp Dijon or wholegrain
  mustard
2 tsps poppy seeds
2 tsps freshly chopped parsley
1 tsps freshly chopped thyme
Freshly ground black pepper
4 spring onions, trimmed and
  shredded
120g/4oz Cheddar cheese, finely
  grated

Cook the pasta in plenty of boiling, salted water for 10 minutes or as directed on the packet. Drain the pasta and cool under running water. When cold drain well. Cook the peas and peppers in boiling water for 5 minutes. Drain and add to the pasta.

Place the oil, vinegar, mustard, poppy seeds, herbs and a little seasoning in a bowl and whisk vigorously until the dressing is thick and pale in colour. Pour the dressing over the pasta. Toss well and chill in the refrigerator until required. Stir the spring onions and cheese into the salad just before serving.

PASTA PRIMAVERA

A classic dish of pasta and young spring vegetables. The flavours should be intense.

Serves 4

INGREDIENTS
460g/1lb pasta of your choice
Salt
225g/8oz asparagus
120g/4oz green beans, trimmed
2 carrots, sliced
60g/2oz butter
60g/2oz mushrooms, sliced
Freshly ground black pepper
3 tomatoes, peeled, seeded and
  chopped
6 spring onions, trimmed and
  sliced
150ml/¼ pint double cream
2 tbsps freshly chopped parsley
2 tbsps freshly chopped tarragon

Cook the pasta in plenty of boiling, salted water for 10 minutes or as directed on the packet. Meanwhile, trim any woody ends from the asparagus and cut each spear diagonally into 2.5cm/1 inch pieces, leaving the tips whole. Blanch the asparagus, beans and carrots for 3 minutes in boiling water, then drain well.

Melt the butter in a large pan and add the blanched vegetables and mushrooms, then sauté for 3 minutes. Stir in the tomatoes and spring onions, then add the cream, seasonings and herbs and bring to the boil. Boil rapidly for a few minutes until the cream thickens slightly. When the pasta is cooked, drain well and add it to the pan, then toss to combine all the ingredients and serve immediately.

PASTA-STUFFED CABBAGE LEAVES

Use a small pasta for the stuffing, or the cabbage leaves will not roll up easily around the mixture.

Serves 4

INGREDIENTS

120g/4oz small pasta shapes for soup
Salt
8 to 12 large cabbage leaves, washed
1 hard-boiled egg, finely chopped
60g/2oz walnuts, chopped
1 tbsp freshly chopped chives
2 tbsps freshly chopped parsley
1 tsp freshly chopped marjoram
Freshly ground black pepper
280ml/½ pint vegetable stock
1 tbsp walnut oil
1 onion, finely chopped
1 green pepper, seeded and chopped
430g/15oz can chopped tomatoes
120g/4oz button mushrooms, chopped
2 tbsps tomato purée
1 bay leaf
Pinch of unrefined sugar

Preheat the oven to 180°F/350°C/Gas Mark 4. Cook the pasta in plenty of boiling, salted water for 8 minutes or as directed on the packet. Remove the thick stem from the base of the cabbage leaves. Blanch the leaves in boiling water for 3 minutes, then drain and refresh them in cold water. When the pasta is cooked, drain it well and mix with the egg, walnuts and herbs, then season lightly. Divide the pasta mixture between the cabbage leaves, fold up to completely enclose the filling and secure with cocktail sticks. Place the cabbage rolls in a shallow ovenproof dish and add the stock. Cover and bake for 40 minutes.

Heat the oil in a frying pan and fry the onion and peppers for 5 minutes or until soft. Stir in the tomatoes, mushrooms, tomato purée, bay leaf and sugar, season to taste and cook gently for 10 minutes. Remove the cabbage parcels from the casserole dish with a slotted spoon and serve with the sauce poured over them.

TRI-COLOURED TAGLIATELLE AND VEGETABLES

This supper dish is subtly flavoured with garlic and rosemary.

Serves 4

INGREDIENTS

225g/8oz tri-coloured tagliatelle (mixture of tomato, spinach and egg pasta)
Salt
60g/2oz butter or margarine
1 large onion, sliced
225g/8oz broccoli florets
2 red peppers, seeded and sliced
2 cloves garlic, crushed
2 tsps freshly chopped rosemary
90g/3oz Cheddar cheese, finely grated
Freshly ground black pepper

Cook the pasta in plenty of boiling, salted water for 10 minutes, or as directed on the packet. Meanwhile, melt half the butter in a frying pan and sauté the onion for 4 minutes, then add the broccoli and peppers and continue to cook for a further 5 minutes, or until all the vegetables are tender.

In a separate pan, heat the garlic, rosemary and the remaining butter gently for a few minutes until the butter melts and the flavours combine. When the pasta is cooked, drain well and return to the pan. Strain the garlic mixture through a sieve on to the pasta – this gives a very subtle hint of garlic and rosemary to the pasta. Add the cooked vegetables and cheese. Season to taste and toss well before serving.

MEATLESS SPAGHETTI BOLOGNESE

I particularly like the flavour of aduki beans, but any cooked beans could be used in this dish.

Serves 2-4

INGREDIENTS

340g/12oz wholewheat spaghetti
4 tbsps olive oil
225g/8oz onions, chopped
1 clove garlic, crushed
430g/15oz can tomatoes, chopped and juice retained
120g/4oz carrots, diced
2 sticks celery, sliced
120g/4oz mushrooms, sliced
1 small red pepper, seeded and diced
1 tbsp freshly chopped basil
1 tbsp freshly chopped oregano
¼ tsp nutmeg
2 tbsps tomato purée
280ml/½ pint stock or water
175g/6oz cooked aduki beans
2 tsps soya flour or cornflour
Salt and freshly ground black pepper
Parmesan cheese

Cook the spaghetti in plenty of boiling, salted water until just tender, or as instructed on the packet.

Heat the olive oil in a large pan and cook the onions and garlic until browned. Add the canned tomatoes with their juice, the carrots, celery, mushrooms, pepper, basil, oregano, nutmeg, tomato purée, and stock. Stir well and simmer for about 20 minutes, or until the vegetables are cooked. Add the cooked beans and heat for a further 5 minutes.

Mix the soya flour with a little water and add it to the sauce. Cook for 2 minutes, until boiling and slightly thickened. Season to taste. Drain the spaghetti and serve, topped with the sauce and a sprinkling of Parmesan cheese.

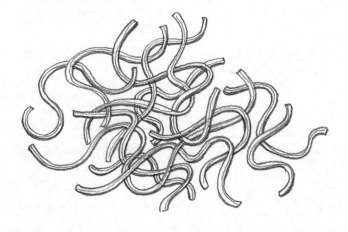

RATATOUILLE LASAGNE

A combination of two favourite dishes – the warmth and brightness of ratatouille and the comfort of a baked lasagne.

Serves 4-6

INGREDIENTS
6 strips green or wholewheat
  lasagne
2-3 tbsps olive oil
2 onions, finely chopped
2 cloves garlic, crushed
1 large aubergine, chopped
1 courgette, thinly sliced
1 green pepper, seeded and
  chopped
1 red pepper, seeded and
  chopped
400g/14oz can chopped tomatoes
2-3 tbsps tomato purée
A little vegetable stock
Salt and freshly ground black
  pepper

White sauce
30g/1oz butter or margarine
30g/1oz wholemeal flour
280ml/½ pint milk

45g/1½oz Parmesan cheese,
  grated
Parsley, to garnish

Preheat the oven to 180°C/350°F/Gas Mark 4. Cook the lasagne in boiling, salted water for 12-15 minutes, then rinse it in cold water to prevent overcooking or sticking.

Heat the oil in a pan and fry the onion and garlic until soft. Add the aubergine, courgette and peppers and cook until soft, then add the tomatoes with their juice and the tomato purée and simmer until the vegetables are tender. It may be necessary to add a little stock at this stage. Season well and set aside until required. Make the white sauce by melting the butter in a small pan. Add the flour and cook for 1 minute, then gradually add the milk, stirring constantly. Bring to the boil and simmer for about 5 minutes. Remove the pan from the heat.

Grease a deep ovenproof dish, and layer the ratatouille and lasagne in it, starting with the ratatouille and finishing with a layer of lasagne. Pour the white sauce over the lasagne and top with the Parmesan cheese. Bake in the preheated oven for 35 minutes until golden. Garnish with parsley before serving.

COURGETTE AND SWEETCORN SAVOURY

A simple but delicious vegetarian pasta bake, and a good way of using up leftover pasta.

Serves 4

INGREDIENTS
1 tbsp oil
1 medium onion, chopped
225g/8oz courgettes, sliced
200g/7oz can sweetcorn, drained
175g/6oz pasta shapes, cooked
Large pinch of dried oregano
1 tbsp tomato purée
Salt and freshly ground black
  pepper

Sauce
30g/1oz butter or margarine
30g/1oz wholewheat flour
280ml/½ pint milk
3 tbsps white wine
60g/2oz strong cheese, grated

Topping
30g/1oz wholemeal breadcrumbs
1 tbsp sunflower seeds

Preheat the oven to 180°C/350°F/Gas Mark 4. Heat the oil in a frying pan and cook the chopped onion until soft. Add the sliced courgettes and brown lightly, then mix in the sweetcorn, cooked pasta, oregano and tomato purée, and stir. Season lightly and transfer the mixture to a greased ovenproof dish.

Make the cheese sauce by melting the butter or margarine and stirring in the flour. Cook gently for a few seconds and then gradually add the milk and wine, stirring all the time, to make a smooth sauce. Bring to the boil, stirring constantly. Add the grated cheese and stir until it melts into the sauce. Remove the pan from the heat and pour the sauce over the vegetable mixture. Top with the breadcrumbs and sunflower seeds. Bake for about 20 minutes in the preheated oven, until browned and bubbling.

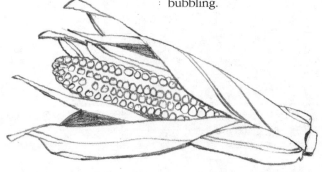

PASTA AND AVOCADO SALAD

A tasty combination of wholesome ingredients producing a filling salad.

Serves 4

INGREDIENTS
225g/8oz pasta shapes
3 tbsps mayonnaise
1 tbsp tahini
1 orange
½ medium red pepper, seeded and chopped
1 medium avocado
Pumpkin seeds to garnish

Cook the pasta in plenty of boiling, salted water until soft, then drain and leave to cool. Mix together the mayonnaise and tahini. Segment the orange and chop it into small pieces, retaining any juice. Chop the pepper.

Stir the mayonnaise mixture, pepper and orange (plus juice) into the pasta. Just before serving, dice the avocado and carefully stir it into the salad. Serve on an oval platter, decorated with pumpkin seeds.

CONCHIGLIE WITH TWO SAUCES

The tomato and mushroom sauces offer a contrast of colours and textures within one dish.

Serves 4

INGREDIENTS
460g/1lb conchiglie (pasta shells), cooked

Tomato sauce
1 large onion, very finely chopped
1 tsp stock powder or half a cube
3 tbsps water
1 clove garlic, crushed
½ tsp dried thyme
Pinch ground rosemary
400g/14oz can tomatoes

Mushroom sauce
250g/9oz oyster mushrooms
30g/1oz butter or margarine
1 tsp stock powder or half a cube
4 tbsps fromage frais
Freshly chopped parsley to garnish

To make the tomato sauce, place the onion, stock powder, water and garlic in a pan and cook very gently for 7-10 minutes, until the onion is soft. Add the thyme and rosemary and cook for 1 minute. Chop the canned tomatoes and add them to the pan together with the tomato juice. Bring to the boil and boil rapidly until the sauce has reduced and thickened.

To make the mushroom sauce, chop the mushrooms finely. Melt the butter in a pan and add the stock powder and mushrooms. Simmer very gently for 10-15 minutes, then remove the pan from the heat and stir in the fromage frais. Heat gently until hot but do not boil.

Divide the pasta between 4 plates and pour the tomato sauce over one half of the pasta and the mushroom sauce over the other half. Sprinkle the chopped parsley between the two sauces, and serve at once.

SPICY ORIENTAL NOODLES

*This is a complete meal in itself, but is also delicious with
sliced cold meat or chicken.*

Serves 4

INGREDIENTS

225g/8oz Chinese noodles
   (medium thickness)
5 tbsps oil
4 carrots
225g/8oz broccoli
12 Chinese dried mushrooms,
   soaked for 30 minutes
4 spring onions, sliced diagonally
1 clove garlic
1-2 tsps chilli sauce, mild or hot
4 tbsps soy sauce
4 tbsps rice wine or dry sherry
2 tsps cornflour

Cook the noodles in boiling salted water for about 4-5 minutes. Drain well, then rinse under hot water to remove excess starch and drain again. Toss with about 1 tbsp of the oil to prevent sticking. Using a large, sharp knife, slice the carrots thinly on the diagonal. Cut the florets off the broccoli and divide into evenly sized but not too small sections. Slice the stalks thinly on the diagonal. If they seem tough, peel them before slicing. Blanch the vegetables in boiling water for about 2 minutes then drain and rinse under cold water to stop further cooking, and leave to drain. Remove and discard the mushroom stems and slice the caps thinly. Set aside with the onions.

Heat a wok and add the remaining oil with the garlic clove. Leave the garlic in the pan while the oil heats and then remove and discard it. Add the carrots and broccoli and stir-fry for about 1 minute. Add the mushrooms and onions and continue to stir-fry, tossing the vegetables in the pan continuously. Combine the chilli sauce, soy sauce, wine and cornflour, mixing well. Pour the mixture over the vegetables and cook until the sauce boils and clears. Toss with the noodles and heat through. Serve immediately.

CAPONATA AND NOODLES

Caponata is a Sicilian dish of aubergines in a well flavoured tomato sauce. This recipe is for a quick caponata mixed with noodles.

Serves 4

INGREDIENTS

1 medium onion, thinly sliced
2 tbsps olive oil
2 cloves garlic, finely chopped
1 large green pepper, seeded and diced
1 large red pepper, seeded and diced
1 medium aubergine, diced
6 tomatoes, peeled, seeded and chopped
1 tbsp tomato purée
3 tbsps red wine
Salt and freshly ground black pepper
120g/4oz green noodles, cooked
90g/3oz grated cheese, Parmesan, Cheddar or a mixture of both

Fry the onion gently in the olive oil for 4 minutes; add the garlic, red and green peppers, aubergine and chopped tomatoes and cook, covered, for a further 5 minutes. Add the tomato purée, wine and salt and pepper to taste, then simmer gently for 10-15 minutes, until the vegetables are almost soft. Remove from the heat and stir in the cooked noodles. Spoon into a shallow flameproof dish and scatter with the grated cheese. Brown under a preheated grill before serving.

TAGLIATELLE WITH RICH TOMATO SAUCE

This is my favourite tomato sauce recipe – it is rich, packed with flavour and satisfying.

Serves 3-4

INGREDIENTS
340g/12oz tagliatelle
3 tbsps olive oil
30g/1oz butter
1 large onion, finely sliced
520g/18oz passata
2 eggs, beaten
60g/2oz Parmesan cheese, freshly grated
6 leaves fresh basil, torn into small pieces
Salt and freshly ground black pepper

Cook the tagliatelle in plenty of boiling, salted water until just tender but still firm. Meanwhile, heat the oil with the butter, add the onion and cook until soft. Stir in the passata, bring to the boil and cook for 5 minutes, until slightly thickened. Cool the sauce very slightly, then stir in the eggs, mixing thoroughly and cooking very gently until they thicken the mixture. Add half the Parmesan, the basil and season with salt and pepper.

Drain the pasta and rinse in boiling water. Drain again and return it to the pan. Add half the sauce and mix well. Serve the remaining sauce over the pasta with the rest of the Parmesan cheese.

COURGETTI SPAGHETTI

This dish is simplicity itself – cook the courgettes until soft so that they blend well with the pasta.

Serves 4

INGREDIENTS
340g/12oz spaghetti
4 tbsps olive oil
60g/2oz butter
4 medium courgettes, trimmed
  and sliced
Salt and freshly ground black
  pepper
45g/1½oz Parmesan cheese,
  freshly grated

Cook the spaghetti in plenty of boiling, salted water until just tender but still firm. Whilst the spaghetti is cooking, heat the oil and butter together in a large frying pan and cook the courgettes until soft. Drain the pasta, rinse in boiling water, then drain again. Return the pasta to the pan, then add the courgettes and all their cooking juices, some salt and pepper and toss together well. Serve with freshly grated Parmesan.

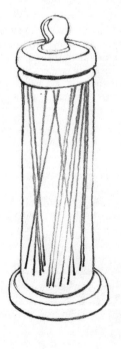

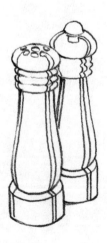

TAGLIATELLE WITH GARLIC AND OIL

This is such a simple recipe but very delicious. I usually serve it as a supper dish with a salad, but it could also be used to accompany a casserole.

Serves 2

INGREDIENTS
280g/10oz green tagliatelle
150ml/¼ pint olive oil
3 cloves garlic, crushed
2 tbsps freshly chopped parsley
Salt and freshly ground black
  pepper

Cook the tagliatelle in lots of boiling, salted water for 10 minutes, or until tender but still firm. Stir occasionally. Meanwhile, make the sauce. Heat the oil in a pan and, when warm, add the garlic. Fry gently until golden brown, then add the chopped parsley, and salt and pepper to taste. Drain the tagliatelle. Add the sauce, and toss to coat the pasta well. Serve hot.

NOODLES IN CURRY SAUCE

This makes an excellent supper dish – warming and tasty but not too heavy.

Serves 4

INGREDIENTS
460g/1lb thin egg noodles
30g/1oz butter or margarine
1 medium onion, finely chopped
1 clove garlic, crushed
2 tsps ground coriander
1 tsp ground fenugreek
1 tsp ground cumin
1 tsp ground turmeric
Pinch of cayenne pepper
1-2 bananas, peeled and sliced
Juice of half a lime
280ml/½ pint stock
280ml/½ pint whole milk yogurt
2 tsps freshly chopped mint
Salt and freshly ground black
    pepper

Cook the noodles in boiling salted water until tender. Rinse under hot water and leave to drain. Melt the butter or margarine in a large pan, and cook the onion until soft, then add the garlic and spices. Cook for 1 minute then add the bananas and lime juice. Cook to soften the bananas slightly, mashing them with a fork. Add the stock, cover and cook for 20 minutes. Blend in a liquidiser or food processor until smooth. Return the sauce to the rinsed-out pan and bring back to the boil. Remove from the heat and add the yogurt, mint and salt and pepper. Pour the sauce over the noodles and toss before serving.

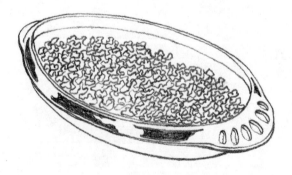

PASTA SPIRALS WITH CREAMY PARSLEY SAUCE

A light supper dish, as delicious by itself as with chicken or fish.

Serves 4

INGREDIENTS

30g/1oz butter or margarine
15g/½oz flour
280ml/½ pint milk
280g/10oz pasta spirals
1 tbsp lemon juice, or 2 tsps
  wine vinegar
1 tbsp freshly chopped parsley
Salt and freshly ground black
  pepper

Melt the butter in a saucepan, then stir in flour. Cook for 1 minute. Remove the pan from the heat, and gradually stir in the milk. Return the pan to the heat, and stir continuously until boiling. Cook for 2 minutes.

Meanwhile, cook the pasta spirals in lots of boiling, salted water for 10 minutes, or until tender but still firm. Rinse in hot water, and drain well. Add the lemon juice and parsley to the sauce and stir well. Season if necessary. Pour the sauce over the pasta and mix well. Serve immediately.

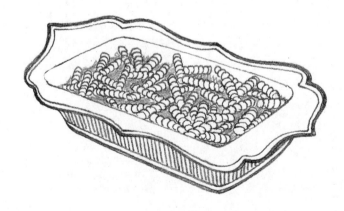

KREPLACH

Kreplach are Jewish ravioli or filled dumplings. They are very similar to Italian ravioli or Chinese wontons. Different fillings are traditionally used at different feasts.

Makes about 50

INGREDIENTS
Kreplach dough
225g/8oz plain flour
½ tsp salt
2 eggs, lightly beaten
2 tbsps cold water
Additional flour for dusting

Potato and Mushroom Filling
10 potatoes, boiled in their skins
2 tbsps butter
2 onions, finely chopped
60g/2oz dried mushrooms,
   soaked in warm water for 10
   minutes
½ tsp salt
½ tsp black pepper

To make the dough, sift the flour and salt into a bowl. Make a well in the centre and add the eggs and water. Gradually incorporate the flour into the eggs until you have a stiff dough. Cover the bowl and let the dough rest while you prepare the filling.

Peel and mash the potatoes. Melt the butter in a frying pan over high heat and sauté the onions until lightly browned. Set aside. Drain the mushrooms and briefly sauté them in the remaining butter. Mix the mashed potatoes, sautéed onions and sautéed mushrooms, then season mixture with salt and pepper.

When ready to fill, roll out the dough until 1.5mm/¹⁄₁₆ inch thick on a lightly floured work surface. Use a ravioli cutter or sharp knife to cut the dough into 5cm/2 inch squares. Place a heaped teaspoon of the filling in the centre of each square. Fold the dough over the filling to form a triangle. Wet your fingers and pinch the edges of the dough firmly together to prevent the filling from escaping. To cook filled kreplach, drop them into boiling, salted water and cook for 15 minutes. Drain well before serving.

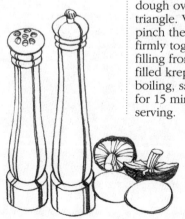

NOODLE KUGEL

These baked noodles are a traditional Jewish accompaniment to a Sabbath stew. They are cooked for a very long time and become light and fragrant. Keep the dish very tightly covered to prevent the noodles from drying out.

Serves 8

INGREDIENTS
30g/1oz breadcrumbs
225g/8oz noodles, cooked and drained
175g/6oz chicken fat or butter
½ tsp salt
½ tsp black pepper
2 eggs, lightly beaten

Preheat the oven to 230°C/450°F/Gas Mark 8. Grease a large casserole or baking dish and sprinkle with the breadcrumbs. Combine the remaining ingredients in a large bowl, then pour into the prepared dish and cover tightly with foil. Bake for 30 minutes, then reduce the heat to 190°C/375°F/Gas Mark 5, and bake for another 30 minutes. Reduce heat further to about 100°C/200°F/Gas Mark ¼ and cook for at least 4 more hours. Serve with stew or other meats.

MACARONI WITH OLIVE SAUCE

Make this dish with green or black olives, or a mixture of both. It is pungent and delicious. I garnish it with chopped anchovies.

Serves 4

INGREDIENTS
340g/12oz macaroni
60g/2oz butter
1 clove garlic, finely chopped
10 olives, pitted and finely chopped
Salt and freshly ground black pepper

Cook the macaroni in boiling, salted water until tender but still firm. Rinse in hot water and set aside to drain. Melt the butter in a saucepan and add the garlic and olives. Cook for 1 minute and then stir in the macaroni. Check the seasoning, adding salt and pepper as necessary. Serve hot.

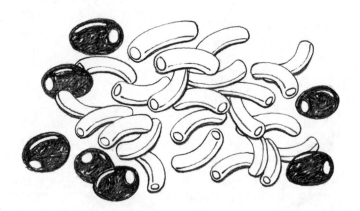

PASTA WITH NUTS, BEANS & CHEESE

There are so many delicious ways of serving pasta with nuts, beans or cheese. Wonderful recipes can be made from a selection of ingredients suitable for most vegetarians and anyone who does not eat meat need never find their food limited or boring if they are inventive with pasta. I often judge a restaurant by the creativity of their vegetarian pasta dishes, despite the fact that I am a meat-eater myself.

Pine Nuts for Pasta

The first time that I appeared on television the presenter asked me where pine nuts come from and I was absolutely floored! My answer – out of a packet! The small, pale nuts, which are technically kernels, are from the stone pine. They have a high oil content and do not keep well becoming rancid, especially in hot weather, so it is advisable to buy them in small quantities and to use them quickly. That said, they have a most wonderful flavour and a delightful texture. I sometimes toast them in a dry frying pan before adding to cooked pasta as this releases even more of their delicate flavour, but take great care not to burn the nuts as they toast very quickly.

Nut Flavoured Pasta

It is perfectly possible to make your own pasta using nuts in the actual dough, but they must be very finely ground to produce good results. I think hazelnuts work best and I use around one third of nuts to two thirds of flour. The dough may become slightly sticky as the nuts start to oil so I find that it is best to rest the pasta after kneading and before it is rolled – about 30 minutes in the refrigerator with the dough in plastic wrap is sufficient. After rolling and cutting I always leave a nut pasta to dry for an hour or so before cooking – this again makes it more manageable.

The appearance of home-made nut pasta is flecked and most attractive. Whilst it might seem a dish suited to a wholewheat flour dough I actually prefer the appearance of the pasta when made with white flour – the flecking from the nuts is then more apparent.

Pasta with Beans

There are several recipes in this chapter for hearty meals with both beans and pasta. These are very filling and, in my opinion, should be served with no starter, a side salad and just some fresh fruit to follow. That said, they make excellent dishes for informal entertaining, especially for large numbers of people. They are usually economical and not too time-consuming to prepare and most, especially the lasagnes, can be eaten with just a fork, which is ideal if guests are having to stand while they eat.

Pasta & Cheese

It is too easy to think of all Italian dishes being topped with Parmesan, and of other dishes being served in a sauce flavoured with grated Cheddar. The Italians actually produce an enormous variety of cheeses, and many of them are used with pasta. Pecorino, bel paese, gorgonzola, mozzarella and ricotta are all delicious when mixed with freshly cooked pasta, and are just a selection of the Italian cheeses that may be used. The Italians are also great ones for mixing their cheeses, and up to four are often used in one dish for a really good flavour.

The Best Parmesan

Fresh Parmesan cheese has only recently become widely available in supermarkets and delicatessens and it is so much fuller in flavour than the grated cheese that is available in little drums. Once you have tasted the cheese 'from the block' it is doubtful that you will ever be happy with anything else.

The highest grade of Parmesan is *Parmigiano Reggiano* and it is never sold under two years old. Mature cheeses are sold between four and five years after making and are very strong. The two year old Parmesan is not only for cooking – it makes the most wonderful table cheese. To keep in prime condition, wrap the cheese very tightly in plastic wrap or foil and keep it in the refrigerator. I always think that a big block of Parmesan is one of the best souvenirs to bring home from an Italian holiday.

Pecorino – a Ewe's Milk Cheese for Pasta

The second most popular cheese for serving with pasta is pecorino. It is very similar to Parmesan but is made from ewe's milk and has a slightly sharp flavour. Pecorino is generally much cheaper than Parmesan as it is sold only eight months after making, so storage costs are much less. Parmesan is a cheese of northern Italy, but pecorino is made in the south and in Sardinia. I think the best pesto is made with a mixture of both.

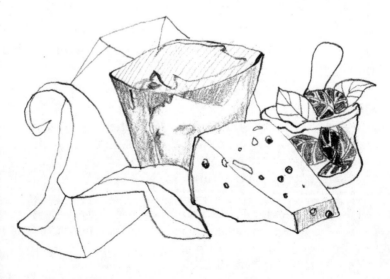

SPAGHETTI WITH SORREL AND CHEESE SAUCE

Sorrel is very similar to spinach, a vegetable that is used extensively in Italian cookery. In this recipe it produces a delicious and unusual dish.

Serves 4

INGREDIENTS

460g/1lb freshly cooked
  spaghetti
120g/4oz sorrel
280ml/½ pint chicken or
  vegetable stock
15g/½oz butter or margarine
1 tbsp flour
120ml/4fl oz double cream
60g/2oz grated pecorino cheese
Salt and freshly ground black
  pepper
Pinch of cayenne pepper
2 hard-boiled eggs, roughly
  chopped
Parmesan cheese

Cook the spaghetti to your liking. Discard any thick stems from the sorrel, then cook the leaves in the stock for 4 minutes. Melt the butter in a separate saucepan, stir in the flour, and cook for 1 minute. Purée the sorrel in its stock in a liquidiser or food processor and gradually add the purée to the saucepan, stirring constantly. Bring to the boil, stirring constantly. Once the sauce has thickened, stir in the cream, cheese, salt and pepper and cayenne pepper and carefully stir in the eggs. Heat the sauce gently, pour it over the drained pasta and add grated Parmesan cheese before serving.

RAVIOLI WITH RICOTTA CHEESE

Ravioli are traditionally filled with meat but cheese fillings are also popular. Ricotta is the best cheese to use and is available in most supermarkets.

Serves 4

INGREDIENTS

Filling
30g/1oz butter or margarine
1 egg yolk
225g/8oz ricotta cheese
60g/2oz Parmesan cheese, grated
2 tbsps freshly chopped parsley
Salt and freshly ground black
  pepper

Dough
250g/9oz strong plain flour
3 eggs, lightly beaten

Tomato sauce
1 tbsp olive oil
30g/1oz bacon
1 small onion, chopped
1 bay leaf
1 tbsp freshly chopped basil
1 tbsp flour
400g/14oz can chopped tomatoes
Salt and freshly ground black
  pepper
1 tbsp double cream

To make the filling, cream the butter, add the egg yolk, and beat well. Beat the ricotta cheese to a cream, and add the butter-egg mixture gradually, beating until smooth. Add the Parmesan cheese, parsley, and salt and pepper to taste. Set to one side.

Prepare the dough by sifting the flour into a bowl. Make a well in the centre, and add the eggs. Work the flour and eggs together with a fork, and then knead the dough by hand until smooth. Wrap in plastic film and leave to rest for 15 minutes in a cool place. Lightly flour a board, and roll the dough out thinly into a rectangle. Cut the dough in half.

Shape the filling into small balls and set them about 4cm/1½ inches apart on one half of the dough. Place the remaining dough on top and cut with a ravioli cutter or small pastry cutter. Seal the edges with a fork or the fingertips. Cook the ravioli in batches in a large, wide pan with plenty of boiling, salted water until tender – about 8 minutes. Remove the ravioli carefully with a slotted spoon.

While the pasta is cooking, prepare the sauce. Heat the oil and fry the bacon and onion until golden. Add the bay leaf and basil, and stir in the flour. Cook for 1 minute, then add tomatoes off the heat stirring continuously, with salt and pepper to taste. Return the pan to the heat and bring to the boil. Cook for 5 minutes, then press the sauce through a sieve. Stir in the cream, and adjust the seasoning to taste. Pour the tomato sauce over the ravioli parcels, toss gently and serve immediately.

FARFALLE WITH CREAMY CHEESE SAUCE

Pasta in cheese sauce has long been a favourite supper dish in our house – the farfalle give this simple dish a most attractive appearance.

Serves 4

INGREDIENTS
15g/½oz butter or margarine
15g/½oz flour
280ml/½ pint milk
60g/2oz Gruyère or Cheddar
  cheese, grated
½ tsp French mustard
280g/10oz farfalle (pasta bows)
1 tbsp grated Parmesan cheese

Heat the butter in a pan. Stir in the flour and cook for 1 minute. Remove the pan from the heat and gradually stir in the milk.

Return the pan to the heat and stir continuously until the sauce boils. Boil for 3 minutes, then stir in the Gruyère or Cheddar cheese and mustard.

Meanwhile, cook the pasta in plenty of boiling salted water for 10 minutes, or until *al dente*. Rinse in hot water and drain well. Pour the cheese sauce over the pasta and toss. Top with a sprinkling of Parmesan cheese. Serve immediately.

TAGLIATELLE WITH BUTTER AND CHEESE

This recipe is simplicity itself – and wickedly delicious.

Serves 4

INGREDIENTS

280g/10oz tagliatelle – preferably a mixture of yellow, green and red tagliatelle
90g/3oz butter
6 tbsps double cream
60g/2oz Parmesan cheese, grated
Salt and freshly ground black pepper

Cook the tagliatelle in a large pan of boiling salted water for 10 minutes, or until just tender, then drain. Meanwhile, place the butter and cream in a pan and stir over a low heat until the butter has melted. Remove from the heat, add half the grated cheese and salt and pepper to taste. Stir into the drained tagliatelle and serve immediately with the remaining cheese on top.

PASTA SHELLS WITH GORGONZOLA CHEESE SAUCE

*Gorgonzola is one of my favourite blue cheeses for cooking –
it has a sharp, tangy flavour. Only a little Parmesan is
required with this dish.*

Serves 4

INGREDIENTS
175g/6oz gorgonzola cheese
4 tbsps milk
30g/1oz butter
3 tbsps double cream
Salt
280g/10oz pasta shells
Parmesan cheese, grated

Heat the gorgonzola, milk and butter gently, in a pan. Sir with a wooden spoon to make a smooth sauce, then stir in the cream, adding a little salt if necessary. Meanwhile, cook the pasta in plenty of boiling salted water for 10 minutes, or until *al dente*. Drain, shaking the colander to remove the excess water. Add the pasta to the hot sauce and toss until well coated. Serve immediately with grated Parmesan cheese on the side.

FONTINA CHEESE RAVIOLI

Fontina is available in most good cheese shops – the next best thing is edam, but the flavour is not the same.

Serves 4

INGREDIENTS
225g/8oz flour
3 eggs
150g/5oz fontina cheese
1 tbsp freshly chopped chives
280ml/½ pint chicken stock
1 sprig rosemary
Salt and freshly ground black
  pepper

Make the pasta by mixing together the flour and 2 of the eggs. Form into a ball then knead until smooth and shiny. Keep in the refrigerator, wrapped, until needed. Cut the cheese into small cubes and mix with the chives.

Roll out the dough thinly on a floured surface and divide into two rectangles. Brush one piece with the remaining egg. Place small piles of the cheese mixture about 4cm/1½ inches apart, then cover with the remaining pasta dough. Cut into ravioli using a small wine glass or pastry cutter and seal the edges. Bring the stock and rosemary to the boil in a saucepan and boil until reduced and thickened. Remove the rosemary and season to taste.

Meanwhile, cook the ravioli in plenty of boiling, salted water for 4-5 minutes. Drain, rinse in hot water and serve with the reduced stock poured over.

LASAGNE WITH FOUR CHEESES

This is a well-flavoured, mixed cheese lasagne, suitable for vegetarians.

Serves 4

INGREDIENTS
225g/8oz green lasagne
60g/2oz butter
3 tbsps plain flour
700ml/1¼ pints milk
45g/1½oz Parmesan cheese, grated
30g/1oz grated Gruyère cheese
30g/1oz mozzarella, diced
30g/1oz pecorino, diced
Salt and freshly ground black pepper and nutmeg

Preheat the oven to 180°C/350°F/Gas Mark 4. Cook the lasagne a few sheets at a time, in plenty of boiling, salted water. Plunge the cooked pasta into cold water and spread out on clean tea-towels.

Melt the butter in a pan, add the flour and stir over a low heat for 1 minute. Remove the pan from the heat and gradually add the milk, stirring well. Bring to the boil, stirring continuously, then add all the cheeses, except 2 tbsps of the Parmesan, and salt, pepper and nutmeg to taste. Stir until the cheeses have melted.

Butter an ovenproof dish and place a layer of lasagne in the bottom. Top with some of the sauce, then continue layering finishing with a layer of sauce. Top with the reserved Parmesan and bake in the preheated oven for about 45 minutes, until well browned. Serve with a green salad.

TAGLIATELLE WITH BLUE CHEESE

The apricots add a touch of sweetness to this dish and provide a dramatic contrast in flavour to the Roquefort.

Serves 4

Ingredients
460g/1lb plain flour
4-5 eggs, lightly beaten
1 tbsp olive oil
120g/4oz blue cheese (Roquefort or Stilton)
150g/5oz dried apricots
280ml/½ pint double cream
4 tbsps milk
Salt and freshly ground black pepper
2 egg yolks
30g/1oz pine nuts
½ bunch chives

Work together the flour and eggs to form a firm ball of dough. Knead lightly then divide into four. Dredge each piece with flour and flour the rollers of a pasta machine. Pass the dough through the machine. Continue rolling the pasta until thin. Thread the dough through the tagliatelle cutter, or cut into thin strips using a sharp knife. Allow to dry for 2 hours.

Bring a large pan of salted water to the boil with the olive oil. Cook the pasta for 2-4 minutes, stirring with a fork. Drain the tagliatelle and rinse in plenty of cold water to prevent sticking. Set aside. Break up the cheese and force it through a sieve using the back of a spoon. Cut the apricots into strips then dice. Slowly heat the cream in a pan. Stir in the cheese and milk then blend until smooth with a whisk or in a liquidiser. Add the tagliatelle and apricots to the hot sauce, and season with salt and pepper. Heat through quickly, so as not to overcook the noodles. Mix the pasta with two forks. Remove from the heat and mix in the egg yolks and pine nuts. Chop the chives finely and sprinkle them over the tagliatelle; serve immediately.

CHEESE AND TOMATO PASTA

The addition of mushrooms gives this tomato sauce just a little extra flavour. Use a mixture of Parmesan and Cheddar, if preferred.

Serves 4

INGREDIENTS
225g/8oz tagliatelle verdi (green)
Salt
1 tbsp vegetable oil
1 onion, chopped
120g/4oz mushrooms, finely
  sliced
1 tbsp tomato purée
400g/14oz can chopped tomatoes
2 tbsps freshly chopped mixed
  herbs
120g/4oz Cheddar cheese, grated
Freshly ground black pepper

Cook the pasta in plenty of boiling salted water for 10 minutes, or as directed on the packet. Meanwhile, heat the oil and cook the onions until they are beginning to soften. Add the mushrooms and fry for 3 minutes, then stir in the tomato purée, tomatoes and herbs, and simmer gently whilst the pasta cooks.

When the pasta is cooked, stir most of the cheese into the tomato sauce. Season to taste with salt and pepper. Drain the pasta and pile it on to a serving dish. Spoon the sauce into the centre and top with the remaining cheese.

OVEN BAKED SPAGHETTI

I make this dish by cooking too much spaghetti one day, and using the left-overs for the base of this simple oven bake.

Serves 4

INGREDIENTS

225g/8oz wholewheat spaghetti, cooked
2 × 400g/14oz cans tomatoes, roughly chopped
1 large onion, grated
1 tbsp freshly chopped oregano
Salt and freshly ground black pepper
120g/4oz Cheddar cheese
30g/1oz Parmesan cheese, grated

Preheat the oven to 180°C/350°F/Gas Mark 4. Grease four individual ovenproof dishes and place a quarter of the cooked spaghetti in each one. Pour the tomatoes over the top, then add the onion and oregano and season well. Slice the cheese finely and arrange it over the top of the spaghetti mixture. Sprinkle with Parmesan and bake in the preheated oven for 30 minutes.

MACARONI AND BLUE CHEESE

Blue cheese and apples combine to make a luxurious macaroni cheese.

Serves 4

INGREDIENTS

340g/12oz wholewheat macaroni
Salt
90g/3oz butter
90g/3oz plain flour
570ml/1 pint milk
1 tbsp freshly chopped tarragon
225g/8oz blue cheese, crumbled
  or grated
Freshly ground black pepper
2 tbsps vegetable oil
2 apples, cored and chopped
2 onions, chopped
1 clove garlic, crushed
Sprig of fresh tarragon, to garnish

Cook the macaroni in plenty of boiling salted water for 12 minutes, or as directed on the packet, then drain well. Meanwhile, melt the butter in a saucepan and stir in the flour, then cook for 1 minute. Remove the pan from the heat and gradually stir in the milk. Return the pan to the heat and cook gently until the sauce boils and thickens, stirring constantly. Add the tarragon and blue cheese and cook until the cheese melts. Season with salt, if needed, and freshly ground pepper.

In a smaller pan, heat the oil and fry the apple, onion and garlic for 5 minutes, until just soft. Mix the apple and onion into the sauce then stir in the drained pasta. Return to the heat and warm the pasta through if necessary. Serve garnished with a sprig of fresh tarragon.

PASTA SPIRALS WITH WALNUTS AND STILTON

Walnuts and Stilton make a perfect partnership of flavours in a delicious pasta sauce.

Serves 4

INGREDIENTS
460g/1lb pasta spirals
Salt
280ml/½ pint double cream
460g/1lb Stilton cheese
120g/4oz walnut halves
Freshly ground black pepper
4 sprigs fresh thyme, to garnish
2 ripe figs, to garnish

Cook the pasta in plenty of boiling salted water for 10 minutes or as directed on the packet. Place the cream in a saucepan and bring to the boil. Boil rapidly for 3 minutes, then crumble in the Stilton cheese and stir until the cheese melts. Stir in the walnut halves and season with pepper.

When the pasta is cooked, drain it well then return it to the pan. Pour the sauce on to the pasta and mix well. Serve garnished with sprigs of thyme and half a ripe fig.

PENNE WITH POPPY SEEDS AND RAISINS

This is a traditional Polish dish, served on Christmas Eve.
Poppy seeds make a delicious crunchy coating on pasta.

Serves 6

INGREDIENTS
Pinch of salt
1 tbsp oil
225g/8oz penne or other pasta
 shapes
150ml/¼ pint double cream
90g/3oz black poppy seeds,
 roughly ground
2 tbsps honey
90g/3oz raisins

Bring plenty of water to the boil
in a large pan with a pinch of
salt. Add the oil and the pasta
and return to the boil. Cook,
uncovered, until tender, about
10-12 minutes. Drain and rinse
the pasta under hot water. If
using immediately, allow to drain
dry. If not, place in a bowl of hot
water to keep moist.

Place the cream in a deep,
heavy-based pan and bring
almost to the boil. When the
cream is almost boiling, mix in
the poppy seeds, honey and
raisins. Cook slowly for about 5
minutes. The mixture should
become thick but still fall off a
spoon easily. Toss the poppy
seed mixture with the drained
pasta and serve hot.

PASTA WITH BASIL AND WALNUT SAUCE

This is a classic sauce for pasta – try it once and you'll be convinced!

Serves 4

INGREDIENTS

120g/4oz shelled walnuts
15 basil leaves
1 small clove garlic
460g/1lb pasta
Olive oil
60g/2oz butter
Salt and freshly ground black
pepper

Pound together the walnuts, basil and garlic in a pestle and mortar until a smooth paste is formed. Cook the pasta in boiling salted water until tender but still firm. Rinse in hot water and set aside to drain.

Heat a little olive oil and the butter together in a pan, add the basil, walnut and garlic mixture and stir well. Add the pasta to the pan, stir well and heat through. Check the seasoning and add salt and pepper as necessary. Serve immediately.

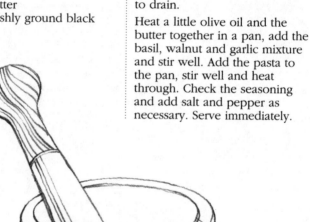

PASTA SHELLS WITH AGLIATA SAUCE

The good thing about pasta shells is that they trap pools of sauce inside them, making wonderful mouthfuls of flavour.

Serves 4

INGREDIENTS
280g/10oz wholewheat or plain pasta shells
Salt and freshly ground black pepper

Sauce
6 tbsps olive oil
3 tbsps roughly chopped parsley
2 cloves garlic
1 tbsp pine kernels
1 tbsp blanched almonds

Cook the pasta shells in a large pan of boiling salted water until just tender. Meanwhile, make the sauce. Place all the ingredients in a liquidiser or food processor and blend until smooth; add salt and pepper to taste. Drain the hot, cooked pasta shells and toss together with the prepared sauce. Serve immediately.

NUTTY SPAGHETTI

A delicious, vegetarian dish which requires no extra seasoning – the peanut butter and lemon juice give plenty of flavour.

Serves 4

INGREDIENTS
225g/8oz spaghetti
1 onion, finely chopped
2 tbsps sunflower oil
2½ tsps curry powder
175ml/6fl oz tomato juice
3 tbsps crunchy peanut butter
1 tbsp lemon juice
Lemon twists and peanuts for
  garnish

Cook the spaghetti in plenty of boiling, salted water until just tender, then drain well. Fry the onion in the oil until golden brown, then stir in the curry powder, tomato juice, peanut butter and lemon juice. Simmer for 5 minutes and then stir the sauce into the spaghetti. Garnish with lemon twists and peanuts before serving.

MACARONI WITH BASIL AND WALNUT SAUCE

*Walnuts give a wonderful flavour to pasta – this dish has
long been a favourite in our house but I have to confess to
adding rather more garlic than is suggested here!*

Serves 4

INGREDIENTS
120g/4oz shelled walnuts
15 basil leaves
¼ clove garlic
460g/1lb macaroni
Salt and freshly ground black
 pepper
1 drop olive oil
60g/2oz butter

Pound together the walnuts, basil
leaves and garlic in a pestle and
mortar until a smooth paste is
formed.

Cook the pasta in boiling salted
water for 10 minutes or until *al
dente*. Rinse in hot water and set
aside to drain.

Heat the olive oil and butter
together in a saucepan, add the
basil, walnut and garlic mixture
and stir well to combine all the
ingredients. Add the drained
macaroni to the pan, stir well
and heat through. Check the
seasoning, add salt and pepper
as necessary, and serve
immediately.

SAUTÉED CHEESE KREPLACH

These cheese-stuffed kreplach are sautéed in butter until lightly browned and then served with sour cream. They are very rich and require only a salad to be served with them.

Serves 6-8

INGREDIENTS
1 batch Kreplach dough (see
    Kreplach recipe)
460g/1lb cottage cheese
60g/2oz grated Cheddar cheese
2 eggs, lightly beaten
½ tsp salt
120g/4oz butter, melted
175g/6oz sour cream or thick
    plain yogurt
½ tsp paprika

Make the kreplach dough. Combine the cottage cheese, Cheddar cheese, eggs and salt in a bowl. Use the mixture to fill the kreplach, then cook the kreplach in boiling, salted water for 15 minutes.

Drain the kreplach on absorbent paper. Melt 2 tablespoons of the butter in a frying pan and sauté a few kreplach until lightly browned – about 3 minutes on each side. As the kreplach are cooked, pile them on to a plate and keep warm. Use remaining butter to sauté rest of kreplach in small batches. Pour some of the sour cream or yogurt over the kreplach, and serve the remainder separately. Sprinkle the kreplach with the paprika and serve.

130

SPAGHETTI WITH PESTO

Pesto is a very versatile sauce – it can be stirred into pasta, soups or any number of sauces and has a delicious, pungent flavour.

Serves 4

INGREDIENTS
5 tbsps olive oil
2 cloves garlic, crushed
2 tbsps pine nuts
120g/4oz fresh basil leaves
3 tbsps Parmesan or pecorino cheese, grated
Salt and freshly ground black pepper
275g/10oz spaghetti

Garnish
Fresh basil

Heat 1 tbsp of the oil over a low heat, add the garlic and pine nuts and cook until the pine nuts are a light golden brown. Finely chop the basil leaves, pine nuts and garlic in a food processor with a metal blade, or in a liquidiser. When smooth, add the remaining oil in a thin stream, blending continuously. Turn the mixture into a bowl and stir in the cheese, adding salt and pepper to taste.

Meanwhile, cook the spaghetti in a large pan of boiling salted water for 10 minutes, or until just tender. Drain, and serve with the pesto tossed through the pasta. Serve with a side dish of grated cheese, and garnish with fresh basil.

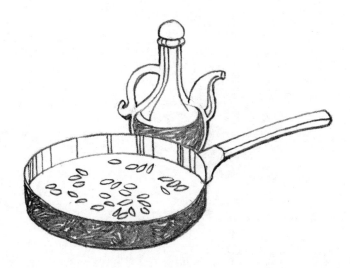

TAGLIATELLE WITH FRESH BASIL SAUCE

This basil sauce is less rich than a traditional pesto, as it does not include any pine nuts. It is very rich, a meal in itself, but may also be served with cold roast meat.

Serves 4

INGREDIENTS
460g/1lb tagliatelle
20 fresh basil leaves
1 clove garlic
30g/1oz Parmesan, grated
60ml/2fl oz olive oil
30g/1oz butter
Salt and freshly ground black
  pepper

Cook the pasta in boiling salted water until tender but still firm. Drain, rinse and then set aside to drain. Pound the basil leaves in a pestle and mortar, then add the garlic and pound until well mixed. Add the Parmesan to a large bowl and whisk in the olive oil. Add the butter to the pasta, place over a gentle heat and add the basil sauce. Stir well with a wooden spoon, and season with salt and pepper. Serve as soon as the pasta is completely heated through.

SPAGHETTI ALLA GENOVESE

The use of less basil and addition of parsley makes this sauce slightly less expensive than the very similar pesto sauce.

Serves 4

INGREDIENTS

30g/1oz fresh basil leaves
15g/½oz fresh parsley
1 clove garlic, crushed
4 tbsps pine nuts or chopped walnuts
60g/2oz Parmesan cheese, grated
Salt and freshly ground black pepper
150ml/¼ pint olive oil
460g/1lb spaghetti, freshly cooked

Combine the basil, parsley, garlic, nuts, cheese and salt and pepper in a food processor or blender and work until finely chopped. With the machine running, pour the oil through the funnel in a thin, steady stream. Process until smooth, with the consistency of mayonnaise. Pour the sauce over the freshly cooked pasta and toss to serve. Serve with additional grated cheese if wished.

133

TAGLIATELLE WITH PINE NUTS

This is a piquant recipe, suitable for vegetarians, but popular with meat eaters too! The pine nuts give a slightly crunchy texture to the dish.

Serves 4

INGREDIENTS
340g/12oz tagliatelle
Salt
90ml/3fl oz olive oil
1 large onion, sliced
1 clove garlic, crushed
120g/4oz pine nuts
400g/14oz can artichoke hearts, drained
2 tbsps freshly chopped parsley
Parmesan cheese

Cook the tagliatelle in plenty of lightly salted boiling water for 10 minutes or until *al dente*. Just before the tagliatelle is cooked, heat the oil in a frying pan and fry the onion and garlic until starting to brown. Add the pine nuts and cook for 1 minute, then add the artichoke hearts and parsley. Heat gently for a few minutes. Drain the tagliatelle well and add it to the pan; toss until the tagliatelle is well coated in the oil. Stir in a generous handful of grated Parmesan. Transfer to a warmed serving dish and scatter with a little more grated Parmesan. Serve immediately.

SPAGHETTI RICE

*This is a filling and unusual dish – I would serve it with a
tossed green salad.*

Serves 4

INGREDIENTS

120g/4oz long grain rice
120g/4oz spaghetti, broken into
 5cm/2 inch pieces
3 tbsps oil
4 tbsps sesame seeds
2 tbsps freshly chopped chives
Salt and freshly ground black
 pepper
430ml/¾ pint chicken, beef or
 vegetable stock
1 tbsp soy sauce
2 tbsps freshly chopped parsley

Rinse the rice and pasta to
remove any starch, and leave to
drain. Heat the oil in a large
frying pan or wok and add the
rice and pasta. Cook over a
moderate heat to brown slightly,
stirring continuously. Add the
sesame seeds and cook until the
rice, pasta and seeds are golden
brown. Add the chives, salt and
pepper, and 280ml/½ pint of
stock. Stir in the soy sauce and
bring to the boil. Cover and cook
for about 20 minutes, or until the
rice and pasta are tender and the
stock is absorbed. Add more of
the reserved stock as necessary.
Do not let the rice and pasta dry
out during cooking. Fluff up the
grains of rice with a fork and
sprinkle with the parsley before
serving.

BEAN SALAD

Crispy bacon adds flavour and texture to this bean and pasta salad. It is an excellent dish to serve as part of a buffet.

Serves 4

INGREDIENTS
225g/8oz macaroni
60g/2oz bacon, rinded and
  chopped
1 onion, chopped
1-2 tbsps wine vinegar
3-4 tbsps olive oil
1 tsp freshly chopped parsley
Salt and freshly ground black
  pepper
425g/15oz can red kidney beans,
  drained
2 sticks celery, sliced diagonally

Cook the macaroni in plenty of salted, boiling water for 10 minutes, or until tender but still firm. Rinse in cold water and drain well. Heat a frying pan and sauté the bacon in its own fat until crisp. Add the onion and cook until soft.

Mix together the vinegar, oil and parsley, and season well. Add the bacon, onion, kidney beans and celery to the macaroni. Pour the dressing over the salad and toss together. Chill briefly before serving.

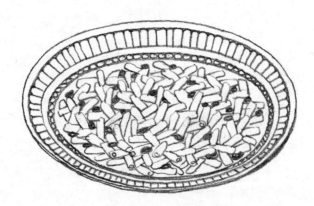

SPAGHETTI WITH KIDNEY BEANS AND PESTO

Pesto is a glorious Italian sauce of basil, garlic and pine nuts blended with olive oil – it often has Parmesan and pecorino cheese added to it as well. Store the sauce in a screw-top jar in the refrigerator for up to a week and add the sauce to pasta, rice and meat dishes.

Serves 4

INGREDIENTS
Pesto Sauce
1 large bunch fresh basil
4 cloves garlic, crushed
3 tbsps pine nuts
150ml/¼ pint extra virgin olive oil
1 tbsp lemon juice
Salt and freshly ground black pepper

225g/8oz spaghetti
Salt and freshly ground black pepper
1 small onion, finely chopped
2 tbsps olive oil
1 clove garlic, crushed
2 tsps pesto sauce
225g/8oz red kidney beans, cooked, or 420g/15oz can, drained

Garnish
Sprigs of fresh basil

Prepare the sauce. Place all the ingredients in a liquidiser or food processor and blend until fairly smooth; the sauce should still retain a little texture.

Bring a large pan of salted water to the boil, add the spaghetti and cook for 10 minutes or until *al dente*. Meanwhile, fry the onion gently in the olive oil for 3 minutes; mix in the garlic and the pesto sauce. Drain the spaghetti thoroughly and add it to the onion and pesto mixture, together with the red kidney beans. Stir over a gentle heat for 1-2 minutes, then serve piping hot, garnished with basil.

BEANY LASAGNE

Lasagne makes an ideal dish for vegetarians. It usually contains lentils but this recipe is made with aduki beans, giving a nutty flavour and texture.

Serves 4-6

INGREDIENTS
8 sheets wholewheat lasagne
1 large onion, finely chopped
1 tbsp olive oil
1-2 cloves garlic, crushed
225g/8oz aduki beans, cooked
1 green pepper, chopped
400g/14oz can chopped tomatoes
1 tbsp tomato purée
1 tsp dried basil
1 tsp dried oregano
Salt and freshly ground black
  pepper

Sauce
30g/1oz margarine or butter
30g/1oz plain wholewheat flour
430ml/¾ pint milk
60g/2oz Cheddar cheese, grated
  (optional)
Salt and freshly ground black
  pepper

Cook the lasagne in a large pan of boiling, salted water for 8-10 minutes. Drain well and spread out on clean tea-towels until required. Cook the onion in the oil until soft but not browned. Add the crushed garlic, then the beans, green pepper, chopped tomatoes, tomato purée and herbs. Season and simmer for about 10 minutes, or until the vegetables are tender.

Preheat the oven to 180°C/350°F/Gas Mark 4. To make the sauce, combine the margarine, flour and cold milk. Gradually bring to the boil, stirring continuously. When thickened, allow to simmer slowly for about 6 minutes, then stir in the cheese and season to taste. Spoon half the bean and vegetable mixture into a greased ovenproof dish and top with half the lasagne. Repeat the layers and top with the cheese sauce. Bake in the preheated oven for 35 minutes, or until golden brown and bubbling. Serve immediately.

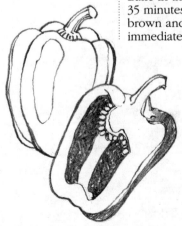

PASTA WITH FISH

Perhaps pasta shells are amongst the most popular of dried pasta shapes because of the Italian passion for pasta with seafood sauces! I have absolutely no proof to support my theory, but there are an amazing number of pasta recipes which include fish.

Quick-Cook Partners

One of the great advantages of meals based on pasta is that they are very quick to prepare and require a relatively short cooking time. Of course there are complicated dishes with intricate garnishes or presentation, and these will take longer than most pasta dishes to prepare, but the vast majority are quick. Fish and seafood are therefore ideal ingredients for pasta sauces as they are so much quicker than the majority of meats to cook, and yet yield the same high protein value in the finished dish.

Clams – A Favourite with Pasta

The first clams that I ever tasted were in a dish of pasta with a seafood sauce. They are molluscs, like oysters and mussels, and have a hinged shell which opens during cooking to reveal the clam inside. Any shells that do not open should, like mussels, be discarded as the clam inside is dead and not to be eaten. Clams are popular throughout the world but especially in the Mediterranean. They are often cultivated in the same pools as oysters and some of the largest clam beds are in France and Portugal. They are ideal molluscs to use in pasta dishes, especially with the thinner shapes such as spaghetti and tagliatelle, as they are relatively small and therefore mix in well. They are also most attractive, having small round shells of a light sandy brown colour.

I always think that mussels look stunning in risottos and paellas, but clams are better in pasta dishes. They are found, or cultivated, in the wet sand of freshwater streams and coasts and therefore require careful washing to remove the sand. When buying live clams this is best done as for mussels. Place them in a large bowl of lightly salted water and sprinkle a little flour or oatmeal on the surface – this encourages the molluscs to clean themselves, flushing the sand out of their shells.

A Garnish Comes into its Own

Anchovies have long been popular the world over as a salty seasoning and garnish for robust dishes which are absolutely loaded with flavour. Many Italian and Mediterranean French recipes are good examples of these strong partnerships of flavours, mixing anchovies with olives, tomatoes, herbs and capers to give pungent and tongue-tingling sauces. Some people do, however, find the anchovies just a little too salty but soaking the fillets in a little milk before use will tone down the flavour.

The recipe for Macaroni Cheese with Anchovies is a classic example of these small fish being used as both a seasoning and a garnish. A word of advice, however, on garnishes. Use a very sharp, smooth bladed knife to cut the anchovy fillets lengthways, making elegant thin strips which look much neater than using the whole fillets for garnish. However, as I am a fan of the strong, salty flavour of the anchovy, I love recipes such as the Penne with Anchovy Sauce, where a paste of the fish is mixed with tomatoes to give a strong, pungent sauce. The anchovies must be mixed with another ingredient as they would be far too strong a flavour by themselves.

Seafood Lasagne – Light but Filling

I often make a seafood lasagne for friends who do not eat meat. I find it an almost perfect dish for entertaining as it is colourful and full of flavour, and just a little unusual. There are two dramatically different lasagne recipes in this chapter, one with a mixture of shellfish and an elegant dish with salmon and fennel. I also often use smoked haddock and chopped hard-boiled eggs. However, a word of advice when serving seafood lasagne, especially when made with fillets of fish. Do try to remove as many bones as possible as, in my experience, people just plough through lasagne expecting all the work to have been done for them. A friend of mine recently had a bone in her throat from my smoked haddock lasagne, which was most embarrassing as she spent the next morning at the local hospital. It isn't always possible to remove all the bones during the preparation, but do warn your friends if you think there might be some in the dish.

TAGLIATELLE WITH EGGS AND LUMPFISH

This is light and sophisticated – add a splash of vodka just before serving for special occasions.

Serves 2, or 4 as a starter

INGREDIENTS
4 small eggs, hard-boiled
225g/8oz red tagliatelle
60g/2oz butter or margarine
Freshly ground black pepper
60g/2oz salmon (keta) or red lumpfish roe

Remove the shells from the hard-boiled eggs, cut in half, and scoop out the yolks with a teaspoon. Push yolks through a sieve. Wash the egg-whites, and cut them into strips.

Cook the tagliatelle in plenty of boiling salted water until *al dente*. Rinse in hot water, and drain well. Heat the butter in a pan, add freshly ground black pepper and the tagliatelle. Add the egg whites, and toss well. Sprinkle the salmon or lumpfish roe over, and top with the sieved egg-yolks. Serve immediately.

TUNA CANNELLONI

Cannelloni are easy to prepare but rinse the tubes well after boiling, to prevent them from sticking together.

Serves 4

Ingredients
12 cannelloni shells

Filling
30g/1oz butter or margarine
1 onion, chopped
90g/3oz mushrooms, chopped
1 stick celery, chopped
1 tbsp flour
150ml/¼ pint milk
4 tbsps double cream
4 tbsps mayonnaise
1 tbsp freshly chopped oregano
200g/7oz can tuna
Salt and freshly ground black
  pepper
3 shallots, chopped
1 egg, lightly beaten

Topping
4 tbsps fresh breadcrumbs
60g/2oz cheese, grated
15g/½oz butter or margarine

Preheat the oven to 190°C/375°F/Mark 5. Cook the cannelloni shells in a large pan of boiling salted water for 15-20 minutes, until tender. Rinse in hot water and drain well.

Meanwhile, melt the butter for the filling in a saucepan. Add the onions and cook until transparent, then add the mushrooms and celery and cook for 5 minutes Stir in the flour and cook until light golden brown. Gradually add the milk, stirring continuously. Bring to the boil and cook for 3 minutes, stirring all the time. Add the cream, mayonnaise, oregano and the undrained flaked tuna. Season with salt and pepper and stir until boiling, then simmer for 3 minutes. Add the shallots and egg, and mix well.

Spoon the mixture into the cannelloni shells and place them in an ovenproof dish. Mix the breadcrumbs and cheese together and scatter over the cannelloni, then dot with butter or margarine. Bake in the preheated oven for 20 minutes. Serve immediately.

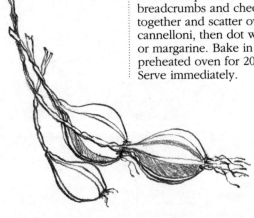

PASTA WITH LEEKS AND MUSSELS

Mussels and leeks combine well in this tasty supper dish.

Serves 6

INGREDIENTS
460g/1lb fresh mussels
120ml/4fl oz white wine
1 shallot, chopped
2 medium-sized leeks
175ml/6fl oz double cream
Salt and freshly ground black
 pepper
460g/1lb pasta spirals
1 tbsp oil
2 slices ham
30g/1oz butter
Freshly chopped chives to
 garnish

Scrub the mussels; remove the beards and wash in several changes of water to remove any sand. In a large, covered saucepan, cook the mussels in the white wine with the chopped shallot for about 5 minutes, over a high heat. Cook, and remove the opened mussels from their shells. Discard any that have not opened. Reserve the cooking liquid.

Quarter each leek lengthways, wash thoroughly, and slice finely. In a covered saucepan, cook the leeks in the cream, with salt and pepper to taste, for 10 minutes over a low heat. Cook the pasta in a large pan of boiling, salted water with the oil. Stir the pasta occasionally as it cooks, to prevent it from sticking. Drain after 5 or 6 minutes and rinse in cold water. Remove any fat or rind from the ham, and slice it into small pieces.

Strain the mussel liquor through a sieve lined with cheesecloth or muslin. Measure out approximately 150ml/¼ pint. Add the shelled mussels and the measured mussel liquor to the cream mixture and cook for 4 minutes, stirring constantly. Melt the butter in a deep frying pan, and reheat the pasta gently with the ham. Season to taste. When the pasta is heated through, add the cream and leek sauce, and serve garnished with the chopped chives.

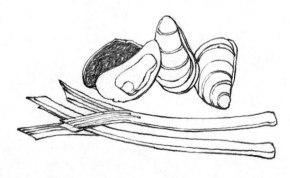

SMOKED HADDOCK WITH PEAS AND PASTA

Smoked haddock is my favourite fish to serve with pasta.

Serves 4

INGREDIENTS
280ml/½ pint milk
225g/8oz smoked haddock fillets, skinned
30g/1oz butter or margarine
30g/1oz flour
1 tbsp freshly chopped chives
1 tbsp freshly chopped parsley
45g/1½oz peas, cooked
1 hard-boiled egg, chopped
Salt and freshly ground black pepper
225g/8oz pasta shells, cooked

Heat the milk gently in a large frying pan which has a tight-fitting lid. Add the fish when the milk is warm, cover the pan and poach the fish gently for about 8 minutes. Check the pan occasionally, adding a little more milk if necessary. When cooked, drain the fish, reserving the milk.

Melt the butter, stir in the flour and heat gently for a few minutes. Add the reserved milk, stirring continuously. Heat until the sauce boils and thickens; if it is too thick, add a little more milk. Add the chives and parsley to the sauce and pour it into a large bowl. Flake the fish, removing any bones. Add the fish to the sauce along with the peas, hard-boiled egg and salt and pepper. Stir well, then add the drained pasta to the sauce mixture and again mix gently to distribute the fish through the pasta and sauce. Return the mixture to a large saucepan and heat gently for 3-4 minutes. Serve immediately.

SHELL PASTA WITH TARAMASALATA

Home-made taramasalata is delicious – used as a sauce for freshly cooked pasta it is rich and most unusual.

Serves 4

INGREDIENTS
Taramasalata
225g/8oz white bread, crusts removed
4 tbsps milk
225g/8oz smoked cod's roe
Half an onion, grated
90ml/3fl oz olive oil
2 tsps lemon juice
Freshly ground black pepper

225g/8oz shell pasta
2 tbsps lemon juice
1 tbsp caviar or black lumpfish roe
10 black olives, pitted and chopped

To make the taramasalata, crumble the bread into a bowl and add the milk. Set aside to soak. Scoop the cod's roe out of its skin, and break it down with a wooden spoon. Squeeze the bread dry in a sieve. Add the onion and bread to the roe, and mix well. Add the oil and lemon juice very gradually, alternating between the two. Beat until smooth and creamy. Add pepper to taste, and salt if necessary.

Cook the pasta shells in lots of boiling, salted water for 10 minutes or until *al dente*. Rinse in hot water, and drain well. Sprinkle the lemon juice over the pasta and toss with the taramasalata. Garnish with caviar or lumpfish roe and black olives. Serve immediately.

CURRIED PRAWN SALAD

I particularly like this prawn pasta salad – the small soup pasta blends well with the prawns to make an evenly textured dish.

Serves 4

INGREDIENTS

2 tbsps olive oil
1 clove garlic, crushed
1 small onion, chopped
1 tbsp curry powder
1 tsp paprika
1 tsp tomato purée
150ml/¼ pint water
2 slices lemon
Salt and freshly ground black pepper
1 tsp apricot jam
280ml/½ pint mayonnaise
225g/8oz small pasta shapes for soup
Juice of half a lemon
225g/8oz cooked prawns, shelled and de-veined

Heat the oil and fry the garlic and onion gently until soft but not browned. Add the curry powder and paprika, and cook over a low heat for 2 minutes. Stir in the tomato purée and water, then add the lemon slices and salt and pepper to taste. Cook slowly for 10 minutes, then stir in the jam and bring to the boil, and simmer for 2 minutes. Strain the mixture and leave to cool. Add the mayonnaise.

Meanwhile, cook the pasta in plenty of boiling, salted water for 10 minutes, or until tender but still firm. Rinse under cold water and drain well. Toss the pasta in the lemon juice, and place in a serving dish. Arrange the prawns on top, and pour the curry sauce over. Toss well. Sprinkle with paprika before serving. Chill briefly if necessary.

NIÇOISE SALAD

A variation on the classic Salade Niçoise. I usually serve this on a bed of crisp lettuce.

Serves 4

INGREDIENTS

225g/8oz penne
200g/7oz can tuna fish, drained
  and flaked
3 tomatoes, quartered
½ cucumber, cut into batons
120g/4oz French beans, cooked
12 black olives, halved and pitted
60g/2oz can anchovy fillets,
  drained, and soaked in milk if
  wished to remove saltiness
Salt and freshly ground black
  pepper
120ml/4fl oz French dressing

Cook the penne in plenty of boiling, salted water until tender, but still firm, about 10 minutes. Rinse in cold water, drain and leave to dry.

Place the flaked tuna in the base of a salad dish. Toss the pasta with the tomatoes, cucumber, French beans, olives and anchovies. Add a little salt and pepper to taste. Pour the French dressing over the salad and mix together with the tuna.

PRAWN SALAD

This recipe makes a very quick lunch dish for two or a starter for four.

Serves 2-4

INGREDIENTS
225g/8oz pasta shells
Juice of 1 lemon
1 tsp paprika
150ml/¼ pint mayonnaise
225g/8oz cooked prawns, shelled
  and de-veined
Salt and freshly ground black
  pepper
1 lettuce
1 cucumber, sliced

Cook the pasta in plenty of boiling, salted water for 10 minutes, or until tender. Drain and rinse under cold water. Shake off any excess water, then place the pasta in a bowl, and add the lemon juice. Leave to cool.

Mix the paprika into the mayonnaise and add the prawns and seasoning, then mix gently. Arrange a bed of lettuce leaves and sliced cucumber in a dish, and pile the pasta into the centre with the prawns on top.

TUNA AND TOMATO SALAD

This makes a substantial salad to serve with a lettuce garnish or as part of a cold buffet.

Serves 4

INGREDIENTS
1 tbsp freshly chopped basil
6 tbsps French dressing
340g/12oz pasta shapes of your choice
6 tomatoes
340g/12oz canned tuna fish, preferably in brine, drained and flaked

Mix the fresh basil with the French dressing in a small jug or bowl. Cook the pasta shapes in a large saucepan of boiling, lightly salted water, until they are tender. This takes about 10 minutes. Rinse the pasta in cold water and drain well, shaking to remove any excess water.

Place the pasta shapes in a large bowl and toss with 3 tablespoons of the French dressing, mixing well to ensure that they are evenly coated. Leave to cool. Slice enough tomatoes to arrange around the outside of the serving dish, and then chop the rest. Place the chopped tomatoes in another bowl and add the remaining French dressing. Pile into the centre of the serving dish.

Add the flaked tuna to the pasta shapes and toss together gently. Pile the pasta and tuna over the chopped tomatoes in the centre of the dish, then arrange the tomato slices around the edge and chill well until required.

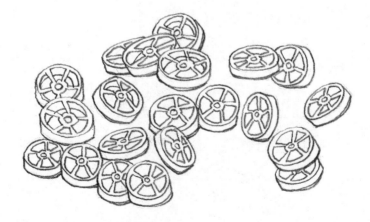

PASTA SHELLS WITH SEAFOOD

I love any dish combining pasta and seafood. The prawns in this become trapped in the pasta shells, producing lovely mouthfuls of flavour!

Serves 4

INGREDIENTS

60g/2oz butter or margarine
2 cloves garlic, crushed
5 tbsps dry white wine
280ml/½ pint single cream
1 tbsp cornflour
2 tbsps water
1 tbsp lemon juice
Salt and freshly ground black
   pepper
280g/10oz pasta shells
460g/1lb raw prawns, shelled
   and de-veined
120g/4oz scallops, cleaned and
   sliced
1 tbsp freshly chopped parsley

Melt the butter in a pan, add the garlic and cook for 1 minute, then add the wine and cream, bring to the boil, and cook for 2 minutes. Mix the cornflour with the water, and pour it into the sauce. Stir until boiling, then add the lemon juice and salt and pepper to taste.

Meanwhile, cook the pasta in plenty of boiling, salted water, until tender – about 10 minutes. Drain, shaking to remove excess water. Add the prawns and scallops to the sauce and cook for 3-4 minutes or until just cooked through. Pour the sauce over the pasta shells, toss and garnish with parsley before serving.

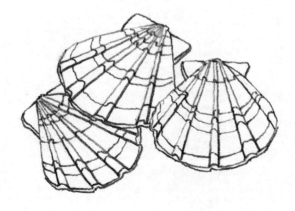

FISH RAVIOLI

*Ravioli stuffed with fish is quite unusual. The lemon sauce
really makes this dish.*

Serves 4

INGREDIENTS

Filling
225g/8oz white fish fillets,
  skinned and boned
1 slice of onion
1 slice of lemon
6 peppercorns
1 bay leaf
1 tbsp lemon juice
280ml/½ pint water
2 eggs, beaten
2 tbsps fresh breadcrumbs
1 spring onion, finely chopped
Salt and freshly ground black
  pepper

Dough
250g/9oz strong plain flour
Pinch of salt
3 eggs, lightly beaten

Lemon sauce
30g/1oz butter or margarine
30g/1oz flour
280ml/½ pint strained cooking
  liquor from the fish
2 tbsps double cream
Salt and freshly ground black
  pepper
2 tbsps lemon juice

Preheat the oven to 180°C/
350°F/Mark 4. Wash and dry the
fish. Place in an ovenproof dish
with the slices of onion and
lemon, the peppercorns, bay leaf,
lemon juice and water. Cover and
cook in the oven for 20 minutes.
Remove the fish with a draining
spoon. Strain the liquor,and set

aside. When the fish is cool, beat
it with the back of a spoon to a
pulp. Add the eggs, breadcrumbs,
spring onion and salt and pepper
to taste then mix well.

Sift the flour into a bowl and add
the salt. Make a well in the
centre, and add the eggs. Work
the flour and eggs together with a
spoon, and then knead by hand,
until a smooth dough is formed.
Leave to rest for 15 minutes.
Lightly flour a board, and roll out
the dough thinly into a rectangle.
Cut the dough in half. Shape the
filling into small balls, and set
them about 4cm/1½ inches apart
on one half of the dough. Place
the other half on top, and cut
with a ravioli cutter or small
pastry cutter. Seal the edges with
a fork. Cook the ravioli in batches
in a large pan of boiling, salted
water until tender – about 8
minutes. Remove carefully with a
draining spoon.

Meanwhile, make the sauce. Melt
the butter in a pan. Stir in the
flour and cook for 30 seconds.
Draw the pan off the heat and
gradually stir in the liquor from
the cooked fish. Return to the
heat and bring to the boil.
Simmer for 4 minutes, stirring
continuously; add the cream and
mix well. Season to taste. Remove
from the heat and gradually stir in
the lemon juice. Do not reboil.
Pour the sauce over the hot
ravioli and serve.

TAGLIATELLE WITH SMOKED SALMON AND CAVIAR

This is affordable luxury! I can never decide which colour tagliatelle I like best in this dish.

Serves 4

INGREDIENTS
225g/8oz green tagliatelle
30g/1oz butter or margarine
Juice of half a lemon
Freshly ground black pepper
90g/3oz smoked salmon, cut into
  strips
2 tbsps double cream
30g/1oz caviar, salmon or red
  lumpfish roe

Garnish
Lemon slices

Cook the tagliatelle in plenty of boiling, salted water for 10 minutes, or until tender but still firm. Rinse under hot water, and drain well.

Heat the butter in a pan, add the lemon juice and freshly ground black pepper, then add the tagliatelle and smoked salmon and toss together. Serve, topped with double cream and a sprinkling of red caviar. Garnish with lemon slices.

SPAGHETTI PESCATORE

This recipe uses a wide selection of shellfish, but you can use whatever is available. The oysters add a touch of luxury but are not essential.

Serves 4

INGREDIENTS
150ml/¼ pint mussels
150ml/¼ pint clams
225g/8oz cod fillets
120g/4oz squid, cleaned
4 king prawns, cooked
4 fresh oysters
225ml/8fl oz dry white wine
700ml/1¼ pints tomato sauce
2 tbsps tomato purée
Half a green pepper, diced
Salt and freshly ground black
   pepper
225g/8oz spaghetti

Prepare the seafood. If using fresh mussels, clean the closed shellfish, removing any beards, and cook in boiling water for 5 minutes until opened. (Discard any that remain closed). Cool and remove the mussels and clams from their shells, keeping a few in shells for garnish if wished. Skin and bone the cod, and cut the fish into 1.25cm/½ inch pieces. Cut the squid into rings.

Heat 2 tbsps of olive oil in a pan, and add the squid. Fry gently until white, then add the wine, the tomato sauce and purée, green pepper, and salt and pepper to taste. Simmer for 20 minutes then add the cod. Simmer for a further 10 minutes, stirring occasionally. Add the clams and mussels and, when the mixture reboils, adjust the seasoning to taste. Add the king prawns and oysters and heat through gently.

Meanwhile, cook the spaghetti in plenty of boiling salted water for 10 minutes, or until tender but still firm. Drain well. Add the seafood sauce, and toss together. Garnish with freshly chopped parsley if wished.

CARRETTIERA WITH PASTA RINGS

*I sometimes add a few cooked peas to this for extra colour,
and a little garlic for extra flavour.*

Serves 4

INGREDIENTS
30g/1oz butter or margarine
120g/4oz mushrooms, sliced
200g/7oz can tuna, flaked
Salt and freshly ground black
  pepper
250g/9oz pasta rings

Heat the butter in a pan, add the mushrooms and cook for 2-3 minutes. Add the flaked tuna and seasoning to taste, then heat gently.

Meanwhile, cook the pasta in plenty of boiling, salted water for 10 minutes, or until tender but still firm. Rinse in hot water and drain well. Add the sauce to the cooked pasta and toss together. Serve immediately.

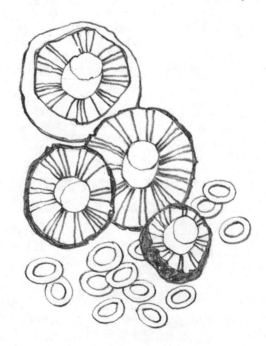

SPAGHETTI MARINARA

*I always enjoy a fish sauce with pasta – it makes a change
from the more traditional meat sauces and is slightly lighter.
This is one of my favourite summer recipes.*

Serves 4

INGREDIENTS
60g/2oz can anchovy fillets
5 tbsps water
5 tbsps dry white wine
1 bay leaf
4 peppercorns
225g/8oz scallops, cleaned and
  sliced
2 tbsps olive oil
2 cloves garlic, crushed
1 tbsp basil
400g/14oz can chopped tomatoes
1 tbsp tomato purée
280g/10oz spaghetti
460g/1lb cooked prawns, shelled
  and de-veined
2 tbsps freshly chopped parsley
Salt and freshly ground black
  pepper

Drain anchovies and cut them into small pieces. Place the water, wine, bay leaf and peppercorns in a pan, and bring to a slow boil. Add the scallops and poach for 2 minutes. Remove the scallops with a slotted spoon and drain.

Heat the oil in a separate pan, add the garlic and basil, and cook for 30 seconds. Add the tomatoes, chopped anchovies and tomato purée. Stir until combined, then cook for 10 minutes.

Meanwhile, bring a large pan of salted water to the boil, add the spaghetti and cook for 10 minutes, or until *al dente*. Drain. Add the prawns and scallops to the sauce, and cook a further 1 minute. Add 1 tbsp of parsley and stir. Season with salt and pepper to taste. Pour the sauce over the spaghetti and serve immediately, sprinkled with the remaining parsley.

CRAB CANNELLONI

An easy way to fill the cannelloni tubes is to place the filling in a piping bag fitted with a large, plain nozzle, then pipe the mixture into the pasta.

Serves 4

INGREDIENTS
12 cannelloni shells

Filling
30g/1oz butter or margarine
3 shallots, chopped
225g/8oz crabmeat
½ tsp Worcestershire sauce
1 tsp Dijon mustard
Salt and freshly ground black
   pepper

Mornay Sauce
30g/1oz butter or margarine
30g/1oz flour
280ml/½ pint milk
30g/1oz Parmesan cheese, grated
Salt and freshly ground black
   pepper

Preheat the oven to
200°C/400°F/Mark 6. Cook the
cannelloni shells in a large pan
of boiling salted water for 15-20
minutes, or until *al dente*. Rinse
in hot water and drain well.

Meanwhile, heat the butter for
the filling in a pan. Add the
shallots, crabmeat, Worcestershire
sauce, mustard and salt and
pepper and stir until heated
through. Fill the cannelloni shells
with the crab mixture and place
them in a greased ovenproof
dish.

Melt the butter for the sauce in a
pan and stir in the flour. Remove
from the heat and gradually add
the milk. Return the pan to the
heat and bring the sauce to the
boil; cook for 3 minutes, stirring
continuously. Stir in half the
cheese until it melts, then season
with salt and pepper. Pour the
sauce over the cannelloni and
sprinkle with the remaining
cheese. Place in the preheated
oven for 10-15 minutes, or under
a hot grill until brown. Serve
immediately.

SEAFOOD WITH EGG NOODLES

This recipe may be made with thread egg noodles or with tagliatelle – I like to use the finer noodles as the dish has a taste of the Orient.

Serves 4

INGREDIENTS

460g/1lb mixed seafood, such as prawns, white fish fillets, squid, clams and mussels
3 large green chillies, seeded and chopped
1 tbsp freshly chopped coriander leaves
2 cloves garlic, crushed
175g/6oz egg noodles
2 tbsps oil
120g/4oz mangetout
120g/4oz baby corn cobs
½ red pepper, sliced
1 tbsp fish sauce
150ml/¼ pint fish stock
1 tbsp lime juice
2 tsps cornflour

Cook the seafood separately in boiling water until cooked through, then drain and set aside. If using squid, score the hoods in a diamond pattern before cutting into pieces. Pound the chillies, coriander and garlic together in a pestle and mortar. Cook the noodles as directed on the packet. Heat the oil in a wok, add the mangetout, baby corn and pepper, and stir-fry for 4 minutes. Add the chilli mixture and fish sauce and cook for 2 minutes. Stir in the fish stock and add the cooked seafood and noodles to the pan. Mix the lime juice and cornflour together. Stir into the wok and cook until boiling and thickened.

PASTA WITH COCKLES

Unless you live on the coast you will probably have difficulty in sourcing cockles in their shells. Use 225-340g/8-12oz shelled cockles, but make certain that they have not been pickled in brine.

Serves 4

INGREDIENTS
460g/1lb cockles
120ml/4fl oz white wine
1 shallot, chopped
300g/11oz spaghetti
60g/2oz butter
1 clove garlic, chopped
1 tbsp freshly chopped parsley
Salt and freshly ground black
    pepper

Place the cockles in a large pan, add the white wine and shallot and place over a high heat. Shake the saucepan frequently until the cockles are open. Remove from the heat and set the pan aside until the cockles are cool enough to handle, then remove them from their shells.

Cook the pasta in boiling salted water until tender but still firm. Rinse in hot water and set aside to drain. Melt the butter in a saucepan, add the garlic, chopped parsley, pasta and the cockles. Season with salt and pepper. Cook until the pasta is heated through. Serve immediately.

SALMON AND FENNEL LASAGNE

Salmon and fennel make a luxurious lasagne for a special occasion.

Serves 4

INGREDIENTS
340g/12oz flour
3 eggs, beaten
30g/1oz butter
15g/½oz flour
280ml/½ pint milk
570g/1¼lbs salmon (in one long piece if possible)
1 tsp fennel seeds
Salt and freshly ground black pepper
225ml/8fl oz fish stock
45g/1½oz Gruyère cheese, grated

Make the dough by mixing together the flour and eggs. Knead well and set the dough aside to rest for 30 minutes. Roll out very thinly into long strips. Part-cook the pasta in boiling salted water for 1 minute. Drain and then lay out on damp tea-towels, without overlapping the strips.

Preheat the oven to 190°C/375°F/Mark 5. Melt the butter in a saucepan and stir in the flour. Cook gently for 1 minute. Remove from the heat and gradually add the milk. Return the pan to the heat and bring the sauce to the boil. Cook for 3 minutes, stirring continuously.

Cut the salmon into long thin slices similar to smoked salmon slices – a very sharp knife with a finely serrated blade is best for this delicate job. Remove all the bones. Butter an ovenproof dish and place some strips of pasta into the base. Build up layers of white sauce, a few fennel seeds, the salmon, salt and pepper and then another layer of pasta. Continue layering, finishing with a layer of pasta. Add the fish stock and then top with the cheese. Cook in the hot oven until the fish stock has been almost completely absorbed, about 20-25 minutes. Serve hot.

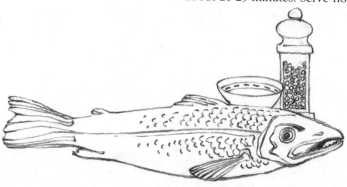

SPAGHETTI WITH CRAB AND BACON

Bacon and crab combine well to make a really flavoursome and luxurious dish.

Serves 4

INGREDIENTS
1 bunch parsley
460g/1lb flour
4 eggs, lightly beaten
225g/8oz bacon, in one piece
1 tbsp olive oil
340g/12oz crab meat
280ml/½ pint double cream
45g/1½oz butter
Salt and freshly ground black
  pepper
Freshly chopped chervil

Trim the leaves off the parsley. Cook for 10 minutes in boiling water then press the parsley through a fine sieve. Reserve the cooking liquid. Purée the parsley with 3 tbsps of the cooking liquid in a liquidiser or food processor. Mix together the flour, eggs and 1½ tbsps of the parsley purée. Knead lightly then form into a ball. Divide the dough into four and form these pieces into balls. Press each ball flat and run it through a pasta machine, until thinly rolled. Pass through the spaghetti cutter, or cut finely with a sharp knife.

Cut the rind off the bacon and cut the meat into strips, and then into small dice. Add the olive oil to a large pan of boiling salted water and cook the spaghetti for 5 minutes. Strain and rinse in hot water. Shred the crab then add it to the cream and heat gently. Meanwhile, heat the butter in a pan and when it bubbles, add the bacon and cook for 3-4 minutes. Add the drained spaghetti, mix well and season with salt and pepper. Place the hot buttered spaghetti around the edge of a serving dish and pour the crab mixture into the centre. Garnish with freshly chopped chervil.

TUNA AND PASTA WITH RED KIDNEY BEANS

This is a substantial salad, suitable for serving as a main course. I sometimes add some diced edam cheese.

Serves 4-6

INGREDIENTS
225g/8oz small pasta shells
225g/8oz can red kidney beans,
  drained and rinsed
120g/4oz button mushrooms,
  quartered
200g/7oz can tuna, drained and
  flaked
4 spring onions, sliced
2 tbsps freshly chopped mixed
  herbs

Dressing
150ml/¼ pint olive oil
3 tbsps white wine vinegar
Squeeze of lemon juice
1 tbsp Dijon mustard
Salt and freshly ground black
  pepper

Cook the pasta shells in boiling salted water with 1 tbsp oil for 10 minutes or until just tender. Rinse under hot water and then place in cold water until ready to use. Mix the dressing ingredients together. Drain the pasta shells. Mix the pasta with the beans, mushrooms, tuna, spring onions and chopped mixed herbs. Pour the dressing over and toss the salad well. Chill for up to 1 hour in the refrigerator before serving.

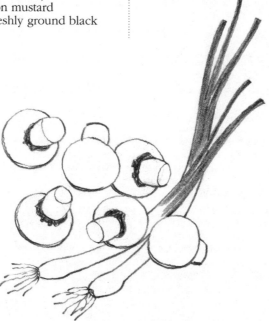

LASAGNE WITH SEAFOOD

This seafood lasagne does not have a sauce topping, so it is covered with foil during baking to prevent it from drying out.

Serves 4-6

INGREDIENTS
460g/1lb plain flour
4 eggs, lightly beaten
4 tbsps olive oil
460g/1lb cockles
680g/1½lb live mussels
460g/1lb prawns
225ml/8fl oz dry white wine
2 shallots, chopped
1 onion, finely chopped
2 cloves garlic, chopped
6 tomatoes, skinned, seeded and crushed
2 tbsps freshly chopped parsley
Salt and freshly ground black pepper
45g/1½oz butter, melted
60g/2oz Gruyère cheese, grated
2tsps freshly chopped chervil

In a bowl, mix together the flour and the eggs, using your fingers to form a dough. Shape into a ball and knead until smooth. Divide the dough into 4 and flatten each piece before passing it through the rollers of a pasta machine. Continue rolling until long, thin strips of pasta are formed. Flour the rollers as necessary during the process. Cut the pasta into small rectangles and leave to dry on clean tea-towels for 30 minutes or so. Cook the lasagne, a few sheets at a time, in plenty of boiling, salted water with 1 tbsp of the olive oil, for 3 minutes. Refresh the lasagne under cold water, then lay it on the tea-towels until required.

Preheat the oven to 200°C/400°F/Mark 6. Wash and scrub the cockles and mussels. Change the water frequently as you wash. Peel the prawns and cut in half if they are very large. Pour the wine into a casserole, add the shallots and cockles and cook, covered, over a high heat until they are open. Remove the cockles with a slotted spoon, then cook the mussels in the same liquid until they are open. Shell both. Fry the onions and garlic in the remaining olive oil in a frying pan. Add the tomatoes and half the chopped parsley. Strain the stock through a sieve lined with cheesecloth or fine muslin. Add the prawns, cockles and mussels, and the cooking liquor, to the pan. Cook over a moderate heat for 15-20 minutes. Season to taste.

Brush an ovenproof baking dish with some of the butter. Layer the sheets of lasagne with the seafood mixture. Brush the pasta with butter each time. Finish with a layer of lasagne and brush it with butter. Top with the cheese and remaining parsley. Cover with foil and bake in the preheated oven for 25 minutes. Remove the foil then brown the top of the lasagne under a grill for 5 minutes. Serve garnished with the chopped chervil.

SOUTH SEA NOODLES

A Chinese dish of rice noodles with an attractive and tasty garnish.

Serves 3-4

INGREDIENTS
2 tbsps Chinese dried shrimps, soaked
225g/8oz Chinese rice flour vermicelli or noodles
4 tbsps oil
2 medium onions, sliced
4 rashers of bacon, rinded and chopped
2 tbsps curry powder
Salt
150ml/¼ pint chicken stock

Garnish
2 tbsps oil
2 cloves garlic, chopped
225g/8oz shelled prawns
1 tbsp soy sauce
1 tbsp Hoisin sauce
1 tbsp pale dry sherry
4 spring onions, chopped
2 tbsps freshly chopped parsley

Drain the Chinese shrimps and chop them. Cook the noodles in boiling, salted water for 3 minutes, then drain and rinse them under cold water. Heat the oil in a wok, add the onion, chopped bacon and dried shrimp. Stir-fry for 1 minute, then add the curry powder and salt. Fry for a further 1 minute. Add the stock and noodles. Stir over the heat for 2-3 minutes, then transfer to a heated serving platter. For the garnish, heat the oil in a small pan, add the garlic and prawns and stir-fry over a high heat for 1 minute. Add the soy and Hoisin sauces, and sherry. Sprinkle with the spring onions and parsley and pour over the noodles to serve.

SINGAPORE FRIED NOODLES

There is plenty of everything in the busy cosmopolitan port of Shanghai and the cooking is a rich mixture of many ingredients.

Serves 4

INGREDIENTS

225g/8oz egg noodles
3 tbsps oil
2 eggs, lightly beaten
Salt and freshly ground black pepper
2 cloves garlic, crushed
1 tsp chilli powder
1 chicken breast, cut into shreds
3 sticks celery, sliced diagonally
2 spring onions, sliced
1 red chilli, seeded and sliced
1 green chilli, seeded and sliced
225g/8oz shrimps, shelled and de-veined
120g/4oz bean sprouts

Garnish

Chilli flowers (carefully cut the end of the chilli into shreds, and soak in cold water until the 'flower' opens)

Soak the noodles in boiling water for 8 minutes, or as directed. Drain and leave to dry on absorbent kitchen paper or a clean tea-towel. Heat a wok, and add 1 tbsp of oil. Add the lightly beaten eggs, and salt and pepper to taste. Stir gently and cook until set. Remove from the wok, and cut into thin strips and keep warm. Add the remaining oil to the wok. When hot, add the garlic and chilli powder and fry for 30 seconds, then add the chicken, celery, spring onions and red and green chillies, and stir-fry for 8 minutes or until chicken has cooked through. Add the noodles, shrimps and bean sprouts, and toss until well mixed and heated through. Serve with the scrambled egg strips on top and garnish with chilli flowers.

FRIED NOODLES WITH PRAWNS

Make certain that the cooked noodles are dry before frying them, so that they do not spatter. This prawn sauce is slightly sweet and sour, and delicious!

Serves 4

INGREDIENTS
225g/8oz fresh noodles
2 tbsps oil
1 red pepper, chopped
1 clove garlic, chopped
20 prawns, peeled and tails left on
1 drop vinegar
60ml/2fl oz orange juice
¼ tsp five-spice powder
225ml/8fl oz fish stock
1 tsp cornflour, combined with a little water
Salt and freshly ground black pepper
Oil for deep-frying

Cook the noodles in boiling, salted water until just tender, then drain and rinse in warm water, and set aside to drain. Heat the oil in a wok and stir-fry the pepper and garlic. Add the prawns and cook until crisp then stir in the vinegar, orange juice, five-spice powder and stock, and cook for 5 minutes. Thicken the sauce by adding the cornflour mixture and stirring continuously until boiling. Season with salt and pepper.

Heat the oil for deep-frying to 180°C/350°F, add the noodles and fry them for 2 minutes, then drain on absorbent kitchen paper. Serve the noodles hot with the prawn sauce.

SHELLFISH IN EGG NOODLE NESTS

A perfect dish to make a big impression on guests! The cockles and mussels may be replaced by prawns or any other shellfish.

Serves 4

INGREDIENTS
120g/4oz Chinese egg noodles
24 mussels, washed and thoroughly rinsed to remove sand
150g/5oz cockles, washed and thoroughly rinsed to remove sand
200ml/7fl oz Chinese wine
1 small courgette
Oil for deep-frying
1 tbsp oil
1 clove garlic, finely chopped
½ tsp finely chopped fresh root ginger
2 leaves Chinese cabbage, shredded
½ tbsp soy sauce
½ tbsp oyster sauce
Salt and freshly ground black pepper

Cook the egg noodles in boiling, lightly salted water until just tender. Rinse under cold water and set aside to drain. Cook the mussels and cockles with the wine in a large covered saucepan for about 3-5 minutes, until the shells have opened, then remove them from their shells. Thickly peel the courgette and slice the peel into thin matchsticks. Discard the flesh and seeds.

Heat the oil in a deep-fat fryer to 180°C/350°F. Make the noodle nests by placing a few noodles on the inside of a small basket fryer or a metal draining spoon. Clamp the noodles in place with a second basket or draining spoon. Plunge each nest into the hot oil and cook for 1-2 minutes until golden brown and crisp. Remove the nest and drain it on absorbent kitchen paper. Repeat the process with the remaining noodles.

Heat the 1 tbsp oil in a wok and stir-fry the garlic, ginger, cockles, mussels and Chinese leaves for 1 minute. Stir in the soy and oyster sauces and season to taste with salt and pepper. Allow the liquid to reduce slightly. Divide the mixture evenly between the fried egg noodle nests.

SEAFOOD CHOW MEIN

*Chow Mein is a wonderful dish of noodles and vegetables in
a rich sauce or gravy. The addition of cockles and mussels,
or any shellfish, makes it very special.*

Serves 4

INGREDIENTS
225g/8oz Chinese noodles
½ green pepper
½ red pepper
1 tbsp oil
1 garlic clove, chopped
½ tsp chopped fresh root ginger
½ spring onion, chopped
175g/6oz cooked mussels
  (shelled weight)
60g/2oz cooked cockles (shelled
  weight)
1 tbsp Chinese wine
2 tbsps soy sauce
Salt and freshly ground black
  pepper

Cook the noodles in boiling,
salted water until just tender,
then rinse them under cold water
and set aside to drain. Cut the
peppers into thin slices. Heat the
oil in a wok and stir-fry the
garlic, ginger, peppers and spring
onion for 1 minute. Stir in the
mussels, cockles, Chinese wine,
soy sauce and the cooked
noodles. Mix together well and
season with salt and pepper.
Serve when heated through
completely.

169

MARINER'S SALAD

A delicious salad with a tangy dressing. Use a selection of your favourite shellfish.

Serves 6

INGREDIENTS

460g/1lb pasta shells, plain and spinach
4 large scallops, cleaned
280ml/½ pint shelled mussels
150ml/¼ pint lemon juice and water mixed
120g/4oz prawns, shelled and de-veined
150ml/¼ pint cockles or small clams, cooked
4 crab sticks, cut into small pieces
4 spring onions, chopped
1 tbsp freshly chopped parsley

Dressing

Grated rind and juice of half a lemon
280ml/½ pint mayonnaise
2 tsps paprika
90ml/3fl oz soured cream or natural yogurt
Salt and freshly ground black pepper

Cook the pasta for 10 minutes in a large pan of boiling salted water. Drain and rinse under hot water, leave in cold water until ready to use.

Cook the scallops and mussels in the lemon juice and water for about 5 minutes or until fairly firm. Cut the scallops into 2 or 3 pieces, depending upon size. Mix the dressing and drain the pasta thoroughly. Mix all the ingredients together and coat completely with dressing. Stir carefully so that the shellfish do not break up. Chill for up to 1 hour before serving.

ITALIAN PASTA PIE

Pasta pies are very filling but very delicious. This one may be scattered with pine nuts before baking, if you wish.

Serves 6-8

INGREDIENTS
570g/1¼lbs puff pastry
460g/1lb fresh spinach, cooked and drained thoroughly
120g/4oz ricotta cheese
1 clove garlic, crushed
Salt and freshly ground black pepper
Generous pinch of grated nutmeg
120g/4oz pasta shapes, cooked until just tender
90g/3oz shelled mussels
1 egg, beaten
1 tbsp freshly chopped basil

To glaze pastry
Beaten egg
Grated Parmesan cheese

Preheat the oven to 190°C/375°F/Mark 5. Roll out two thirds of the puff pastry quite thinly and use to line the sides and base of a loose-bottomed 17.5cm/7-inch round cake tin. Press the pastry carefully into the shape of the tin, avoiding any cracks or splits. Roll out the remaining pastry to a circle large enough to generously cover the top of the cake tin.

Mix the spinach with the ricotta cheese, garlic, salt and pepper, nutmeg to taste, the cooked pasta, mussels and the beaten egg and basil. Spoon the filling into the pastry-lined tin. Brush the rim of the pastry with some of the beaten egg and lay the pastry lid over the filling and press the edges together to seal. Trim off any the excess pastry and pinch the edges decoratively. Cut shapes from the pastry trimmings to decorate the top of the pie. Glaze with the remaining beaten egg and sprinkle with grated Parmesan cheese.

Bake in the oven for 45 minutes, then cover with a piece of foil and cook for a further 20 minutes. Unmould the pie carefully and serve hot, cut into wedges.

PENNE WITH ANCHOVY SAUCE

This is an unusual sauce but one which makes good use of the favourite Italian ingredient, the anchovy.

Serves 4

INGREDIENTS
6-8 anchovy fillets, drained
2 tbsps olive oil
400g/14oz can chopped tomatoes
3 tbsps freshly chopped parsley
Freshly ground black pepper
280g/10oz penne
30g/1oz butter or margarine, melted
30g/1oz Parmesan cheese

Chop the anchovies and cook them briefly in the oil, stirring until they break up into a paste. Add the chopped tomatoes with the parsley and freshly ground black pepper to taste. Bring to the boil and simmer, uncovered for 10 minutes.

Meanwhile, cook the penne in plenty of boiling salted water for 10 minutes, or until *al dente*. Rinse in hot water and drain well; then toss the penne in the melted butter. Combine the sauce with the pasta, sprinkle with a little extra chopped parsley, and serve immediately with grated Parmesan cheese.

MACARONI CHEESE WITH ANCHOVIES

I love anchovies and add them to all sorts of dishes – they give an extra dimension to macaroni cheese.

Serves 4

INGREDIENTS
60g/2oz can anchovy fillets
225g/8oz macaroni
60g/2oz butter or margarine
60g/2oz flour
570ml/1 pint milk
½ tsp mustard powder
175g/6oz Gruyère or Cheddar
  cheese, grated
Salt and freshly ground black
  pepper

Drain the anchovies, reserving 4-5 fillets to slice to make a thin lattice over the dish. Chop the rest finely. Cook the macaroni in plenty of boiling salted water for 10 minutes, or until tender but still firm. Rinse in hot water and drain well.

Meanwhile, melt the butter in a pan, then stir in the flour and cook for 1 minute. Remove from the heat and gradually stir in the milk. Return to the heat and bring to the boil, stirring continuously. Simmer for 3 minutes, then stir in the mustard, anchovies, and half the cheese. Season with salt and pepper to taste then stir in the macaroni, and pour into an ovenproof dish. Scatter the remaining cheese over the top, and make a lattice with the remaining anchovies. Brown under a hot grill and serve immediately.

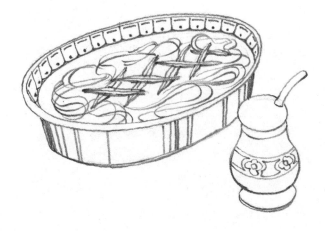

SPAGHETTI ALLA VONGOLE

Vongole is the Italian word for clams, and this is a classic Neapolitan pasta dish.

Serves 4-6

INGREDIENTS
6 tbsps olive oil
900g/2lbs live clams
460g/1lb spaghetti
2 × 400g/14oz cans chopped
  tomatoes
2 cloves garlic, crushed
Salt and freshly ground black
  pepper
2 tbsps freshly chopped parsley

Heat the oil in a large pan, add the clams, cover and cook until the shells open, shaking the pan from time to time. Discard the shells and set the clams aside. Boil the cooking liquor from the clams to reduce by half, then strain through a fine sieve lined with muslin.

Cook the spaghetti in plenty of boiling, salted water until just tender but still firm. Drain, rinse in boiling water then drain again. Meanwhile, add the tomatoes and garlic to the reduced clam liquor in a pan and heat through, seasoning to taste. Add the clams and reheat them gently, then add the hot spaghetti and toss until well mixed. Serve, garnished with plenty of freshly chopped parsley.

GARNISHED NOODLES

I think that noodles are far more interesting to serve with a Chinese meal than rice. Nori is a Japanese seaweed dried in thin sheets.

Serves 4

INGREDIENTS
Sauce
3 tbsps white wine vinegar
3 tbsps soy sauce
2 tsps sugar
150ml/¼ pint chicken stock or
   dashi
460g/1lb Chinese noodles

Garnishes
Cucumber, diced
120g/4oz small peeled prawns
Celery leaves
2 sheets nori, toasted and
   crumbled or shredded

Combine the vinegar, soy sauce, sugar and stock in a pan and bring to the boil. Remove from the heat and keep warm. Cook the noodles in plenty of boiling water for about 5 minutes, until tender. Drain in a colander and rinse with hot water. Divide the noodles among 4 serving dishes and arrange the garnishes on top. Pour the sauce over and serve.

PASTA WITH CHICKEN

Although chicken is one of the most versatile of foods I have found it to be comparatively, and surprisingly, difficult to assemble an interesting selection of recipes for pasta and chicken. There seem to be so many seafood and meat recipes to choose from, but only a limited number for poultry. Perhaps everyone makes up such recipes as they go along, and never stop to write them down? However, I am certain that the selection which follows will set your taste-buds tingling.

Chicken, the Perfect Ingredient

Chicken is exceptionally versatile because it has a light flavour of its own which readily marries and mixes with so many other ingredients. Chicken is as happy in a mild creamy sauce with just a flavouring of saffron as it is mixed with olives, anchovies and peppers. The ability of chicken to perform as a culinary tonic water, the perfect mixer, is amply illustrated by the number of classic chicken recipes that occur in just about every major cuisine of the world.

Light & Dark Meat for Flavour

Although it is easy and convenient to buy chicken pieces or joints it is much more expensive than buying a whole bird, and also limits the flavour that you will get from the meat. The whitest meat from a chicken is the breast, which is the most luscious part with less fat and bone than other joints and very little wastage. However, I often find that chicken breasts can be dry and tasteless, and that they are very easy to overcook. My favourite joint from the chicken is the thigh, which is darker meat of a more intense flavour, and it is also considerably cheaper than the breast.

All the recipes that follow require boneless chicken (you wouldn't want great drumsticks mixed into a dish of pasta shapes) and boneless thighs are available in most supermarkets, although you will pay more for them than the meat on the bone. When I am shopping for a recipe which requires boneless chicken meat I always buy a mixture of breasts and thighs to get a good balance of flavours between the light and dark meat.

Pasta Suppers with Left-Over Chicken

Many people find left-over meals to be dull and definitely second rate, and yet I find that easy supper dishes made with cooked chicken and pasta offer really satisfying and tasty meals. The cooked chicken is usually reheated in a sauce so the finished dish can be as flavoursome and inventive as your sauce making. One of my favourite dishes is the Chicken Bolognese with Nuts; the cashews and walnuts make what might otherwise be a pale imitation of a classic dish into a tasty recipe in its own right. Another of my favourite combinations is a mixture of chicken, pasta and grapes – hot as Chicken Pasta Veronique, or cold as Chicken & Grape Pasta Salad.

Pasta & Chicken the Chinese Way

Pasta and chicken are both very popular in Chinese cookery. The pasta is usually noodles so it is best to shred the chicken finely to go into dishes, so that it blends with the noodles instead of dominating them. I like to cook fresh chicken with ginger, or with peaches and spring onions, or even with plenty of mixed oriental vegetables in a Chicken Chop Suey, and I find that cooked chicken may be made into wonderful supper dishes by mixing it with a simple stir-fry sauce and noodles, or prawns and nuts for a more elaborate all-in-one noodle dish.

Chicken Stuffed Tortellini

Tortellini are available dried in most supermarkets and delicatessens and they are an excellent stand-by to keep in the store-cupboard. However, the commercial pasta bears almost no resemblance to tortellini made at home which, although a fiddle to fold, are well worth the effort of making. I think that the chicken and spinach filling used in this chapter is one of the nicest that I have tried.

Tortellini are folded to resemble little hats or circles when home-made. The folding of the hats is an art – I usually make the circles, as directed in the recipe in this chapter! However no tortellini, no matter how delicious their filling or how neatly they are folded, are really enjoyable without a sauce and the creamy mushroom sauce with the chicken stuffed tortellini makes a very pleasant change from the more traditional tomato accompaniment.

SPAGHETTI WITH CHICKEN BOLOGNESE AND NUTS

Chicken and nuts. Pasta and nuts. Both are winning combinations. All three ingredients make a very special spaghetti sauce.

Serves 4

INGREDIENTS

Sauce

1 medium onion, finely chopped
1 clove garlic, finely chopped
2 tbsps olive oil
200ml/7fl oz red wine
2 tbsps tomato purée
1 tbsp fresh chopped thyme
Salt and freshly ground black pepper
225g/8oz cooked chicken, finely chopped
6 tomatoes, seeded and chopped
1 tsp pesto sauce
30g/1oz cashew nuts, chopped
30g/1oz walnuts, chopped

340g/12oz spaghetti, plain or wholewheat

Garnish

Chopped walnuts

Fry the onion and garlic in the olive oil for 3 minutes. Add the red wine, tomato purée, thyme and salt and pepper to taste. Bring to the boil and simmer for 10 minutes. Add the chopped chicken, tomatoes, pesto sauce, cashew nuts and walnuts, then simmer the sauce for a further few minutes.

Meanwhile, cook the spaghetti in boiling, salted water for 8-10 minutes, until just tender. Drain the spaghetti thoroughly. If the sauce is too thick for your liking, thin it down with a little hot stock or water. Pile the cooked spaghetti into a serving dish and spoon the sauce over the top. Sprinkle with extra chopped walnuts and serve immediately.

CHICKEN LASAGNE

Lasagne is traditionally made with beef and topped with a white sauce. This lighter version is made with chicken and stock.

Serves 4

INGREDIENTS
400g/14oz flour
3 eggs, beaten
60g/2oz butter
1 medium onion, chopped
1 clove garlic, chopped
570g/1¼lbs minced chicken
2 mushrooms, chopped
60ml/2fl oz white wine
520ml/18fl oz chicken stock
Sprig thyme
1 bay leaf
1 tbsp tomato purée
Salt and freshly ground black
    pepper
45g/1½oz Parmesan cheese,
    grated

Make the dough by mixing together the flour and eggs. Form into a ball, knead lightly then coat with a little flour, wrap and place in the refrigerator for 30 minutes.

Heat half the butter in a frying pan and cook the onion and garlic until lightly browned. Stir in the chicken and mushrooms and cook for 2 minutes. Add the white wine, allow it to reduce and stir in 280ml/½ pint of the chicken stock. Add the thyme, bay leaf and tomato purée, and cook until the liquid has reduced by half. Remove the thyme and bay leaf and season with salt and pepper.

Preheat the oven to 180°C/350°F/Mark 4. Roll the dough out thinly or pass it through a pasta machine and cut into even-sized rectangular strips. Cook for 1 minute in boiling salted water, then rinse under hot water and set aside to dry slightly on a slightly damp tea-towel. Grease an ovenproof dish with the remaining butter and lay strips of pasta in the base. Cover each layer of pasta with a layer of the chicken sauce and continue layering until all the pasta and sauce has been used. Pour the remaining chicken stock into the dish, sprinkle over the grated Parmesan cheese and cook in the preheated oven until the juices have almost entirely evaporated – about 40 minutes. Serve piping hot from the oven.

MACARONI WITH CREAMY CHICKEN SAUCE

The addition of even a little chopped chicken turns a supper dish of macaroni cheese into a substantial main course.

Serves 4

INGREDIENTS
1 tbsp olive oil
120g/4oz boneless chicken breast
225g/8oz macaroni
60g/2oz butter
30g/1oz flour
570ml/1 pint milk
Salt and freshly ground black
    pepper
120g/4oz mozzarella cheese,
    grated or thinly sliced

Heat the oil in a frying pan and gently fry the chicken for 10 minutes, or until cooked through. Allow to cool, then shred the chicken. Cook the macaroni in plenty of boiling salted water for 10 minutes, or until *al dente*, then rinse in hot water and drain well.

Meanwhile, heat the butter in a pan, stir in the flour and cook for 1 minute. Draw off the heat and gradually add the milk, stirring all the time. Bring the sauce to the boil, stirring continuously, and cook for 3 minutes. Add the chicken, macaroni, and salt and pepper to taste, and mix well. Pour the mixture into an ovenproof dish and top with the cheese. Cook under a preheated grill until golden brown, then serve immediately.

LASAGNE ROLLS

Roll your own cannelloni!

Serves 4

INGREDIENTS
2 tsps vegetable oil
8 sheets lasagne
60g/2oz button mushrooms,
  sliced
225g/8oz boneless chicken breast
30g/1oz butter or margarine
30g/1oz plain flour
150ml/¼ pint milk
120g/4oz Gruyère or Cheddar
  cheese, grated
Salt and freshly ground black
  pepper

Fill a large saucepan two thirds full with salted water. Add the oil and bring to the boil. Add 1 sheet of lasagne, wait about 2 minutes, then add another sheet. Cook only a few at a time and when tender, after about 6-7 minutes, remove from the boiling water and rinse under cold water. Allow to drain on a tea-towel. Repeat this process until all the lasagne is cooked.

Slice the mushrooms, and slice the chicken breast into thin strips. Melt half the butter in a small frying pan and fry the mushrooms and the chicken for about 10 minutes, until the chicken is just cooked. In a small saucepan, melt the remaining butter. Stir in the flour and heat gently for 1 minute. Remove the pan from the heat and gradually add the milk, stirring well. Return the pan to the heat and bring to the boil, stirring all the time. Cook for 3 minutes. Pour the sauce over the chicken and mushrooms. Add half the cheese and mix well then season to taste.

Lay the sheets of lasagne on a board and divide the chicken mixture equally between them. Spread the chicken mixture over each lasagne sheet and roll up lengthways, like a Swiss roll. Place the rolls in an ovenproof dish. Sprinkle with the remaining cheese and grill under a pre-heated moderate grill, until the cheese is bubbly and golden brown.

SHANGHAI NOODLES

Noodles are more popular in the north of China than in the rice growing areas of the south. In Shanghai there is plenty of everything.

Serves 4

INGREDIENTS
3 tbsps oil
120g/4oz chicken breasts
460g/1lb thick Shanghai noodles
 or tagliatelle
120g/4oz Chinese leaves,
 shredded
4 spring onions, thinly sliced
2 tbsps soy sauce
Freshly ground black pepper
Dash of sesame oil

Heat the oil in a wok and add the chicken cut into thin shreds. Stir-fry for 2-3 minutes. Meanwhile, cook the noodles in boiling salted water until just tender, about 6-8 minutes. Drain in a colander and rinse under hot water. Toss in the colander to drain and leave to dry. Add the shredded Chinese leaves and spring onions to the chicken in the wok along with the soy sauce, pepper and sesame oil. Cook for about 1 minute then toss in the cooked noodles. Stir well and heat through. Serve immediately.

MEXICAN CHICKEN SALAD

Add some chilli sauce to the dressing instead of vinegar for a spicier Mexican flavour.

Serves 4

INGREDIENTS
225g/8oz small pasta shapes for soup
225g/8oz cooked chicken, shredded
200g/7oz can sweetcorn kernels, drained
1 stick celery, sliced
1 red pepper, diced
1 green pepper, diced

Dressing
1 tbsp mayonnaise
2 tbsps white wine vinegar
Salt and freshly ground black pepper

Cook the pasta in plenty of boiling, salted water until just tender, about 6-8 minutes. Drain well, and leave to cool. Meanwhile, combine the mayonnaise with the vinegar and salt and pepper to make a dressing. When the pasta is cool, add the chicken, sweetcorn, celery and peppers. Toss together well and serve with dressing.

HERB RAVIOLI WITH CHICKEN STOCK

Home-made ravioli dough is coated with fresh herbs and cooked in a chicken stock flavoured with rosemary. This recipe is a soup and pasta dish combined.

Serves 4

INGREDIENTS
175g/6oz flour
1 egg, beaten
1 bunch chervil, washed and chopped
1 bunch parsley, washed and chopped
1 litre/1¾ pints chicken stock
1 tsp dried rosemary
Salt and freshly ground black pepper

Make the dough by mixing together the flour, a good pinch of salt and the egg in a large bowl. Set aside to rest for 30 minutes. Pass the dough through a pasta machine, flouring both sides of the dough as it goes through the rollers to prevent sticking. Cut the dough into long strips. Alternatively, roll the dough thinly with a rolling pin and cut into strips. Spread out half of the strips on to your work surface and sprinkle over the chervil and parsley. Place the remaining strips on top, press down well all along the strips with your fingers and then once again run the strips through the rollers of the pasta machine, or re-roll with a rolling pin.

Heat the stock and rosemary together in a saucepan until just boiling. Season with salt and pepper. Cut the dough into the desired ravioli shapes. Cook in the boiling stock for 2-4 minutes. Serve very hot in shallow soup plates.

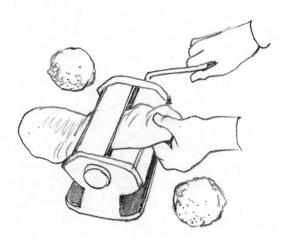

TORTELLINI

Tortellini are like little hats of filled pasta and are always served with a sauce – I tried them once without and they were very dry.

Serves 4

INGREDIENTS

Dough
150g/5oz strong plain flour
Pinch of salt
1 tbsp water
1 tbsp oil
3 eggs, lightly beaten

Filling
30g/1oz cream cheese
1 cooked chicken breast, finely diced
1 slice ham, shredded
2 spinach leaves, stalks removed, cooked and finely chopped
1 tbsp grated Parmesan cheese
1 egg, beaten
Salt and freshly ground black pepper

Sauce
225ml/8fl oz double cream
120g/4oz mushrooms, sliced
30g/1oz Parmesan cheese, grated
1 tbsp freshly chopped parsley
Salt and freshly ground black pepper

Prepare the filling. Beat the cream cheese until soft and smooth, then add the chicken, ham, spinach and Parmesan cheese, and mix well. Add the egg gradually, and salt and pepper to taste. Set aside until required.

To make the pasta dough, sift the flour and salt into a bowl and make a well in the centre. Mix the water, oil and lightly beaten egg together, and pour into the well, working in the flour a little at a time. Continue until the mixture comes together in a ball. Knead on a lightly floured surface for 5 minutes, or until smooth and elastic. Place in a bowl, cover with a cloth, and leave to stand for 15 minutes.

Roll the dough out as thinly as possible. Cut into circles using a 5cm/2 inch cutter and place half a teaspoon of filling in the centre of each. Fold in half, pressing the edges together firmly. Wrap around forefinger, and press the ends together.

Cook the tortellini in batches in a large pan of boiling salted water for about 10 minutes until tender, stirring occasionally. Drain.

While the tortellini are cooking make the sauce. Gently heat the cream in a pan. Add the mushrooms, Parmesan, parsley and salt and pepper to taste. Gently cook for 3 minutes. Toss the sauce together with the tortellini. Serve immediately.

CHINESE CHICKEN WITH PASTA

This is not a classic Chinese dish, but it is delicious!

Serves 2

INGREDIENTS
2 boneless chicken breasts, skinned
Grated rind and juice of half a lime,
Small piece fresh root ginger, peeled and finely grated
1 clove garlic, crushed
1 tbsp sesame oil
2 tbsps light soy sauce
175g/6oz tagliatelle
30g/1oz butter
Salt and freshly ground black pepper
Freshly chopped parsley to garnish

Place the chicken breasts in a small ovenproof casserole dish. Mix together the rind and juice of the lime, the ginger, garlic, sesame oil and soy sauce and pour the sauce over the chicken. Leave in a cool place to marinate for 4 hours.

Preheat the oven to 190°C/375°F/Mark 5. Bake the chicken in the marinade, uncovered, in the hot oven for 30 minutes, turning once. Increase the heat to 220°C/425°F/Mark 7 for the final 5 minutes of the cooking time.

Whilst the chicken is baking, cook the pasta in plenty of boiling, salted water until tender but still firm. Drain, then rinse in boiling water and drain again. Melt the butter in the pasta pan, add the tagliatelle and some freshly ground black pepper and toss until mixed. Slice the cooked chicken breasts and add them to the pasta with any remaining sauce. Add extra butter if necessary and serve immediately garnished with chopped parsley.

CHICKEN PASTA VERONIQUE

Sole is often served in a white wine sauce, garnished with grapes in a dish called Sole Veronique. The combination of sauce and garnish works just as well with chicken and pasta.

Serves 4

INGREDIENTS
30g/1oz butter
2 tbsps olive oil
4 small part-boned chicken
  breasts, skinned
3-4 spring onions, finely sliced
150ml/¼ pint dry white wine
150ml/¼ pint double cream
Salt and freshly ground black
  pepper
340g/12oz tagliatelle
Lemon juice
120g/4oz grapes, black or green,
  seeded and halved, to garnish

Preheat the oven to 190°C/375°F/Mark 5. Heat the butter with 1 tablespoon of the olive oil in a frying pan, then add the chicken and cook until well browned on all sides. Remove the chicken from the pan with a slotted spoon and transfer it to an ovenproof dish. Cook the spring onions briefly in the fat remaining in the pan until just soft, then add the wine and cream and heat gently. Season with a little salt and pepper, then pour the sauce over the chicken and bake in the preheated oven for 20-30 minutes, until the chicken is cooked through.

Meanwhile, cook the pasta in plenty of boiling, salted water until just tender but still firm, about 10 minutes. Drain, then rinse in boiling water and drain again. Return the pasta to the pan, add the remaining olive oil and some black pepper and toss together. Transfer the pasta to a warm serving dish and arrange the cooked chicken in the centre of it. Season the sauce if necessary, adding a squeeze of lemon juice to taste, then spoon the sauce over the chicken. Garnish with the grapes before serving.

NOODLES WITH CHICKEN AND PRAWNS

This recipe would serve four as part of a Chinese meal but would also make a filling supper dish for two people.

Serves 2-4

INGREDIENTS
225g/8oz Chinese noodles
3 tbsps oil
2 shallots, finely chopped
1 clove garlic, crushed
225g/8oz chicken, skinned, boned and cut into small pieces
2 courgettes, cut in strips
3 tbsps soy sauce
60g/2oz cooked peeled prawns

Garnish
4 spring onions, finely shredded
1 red chilli, seeded and finely shredded

Cook the noodles in boiling, salted water until just tender. Drain and rinse under hot water and toss in a colander to remove excess water. Heat the oil in a wok or heavy-based frying pan and cook the shallots and garlic until softened. Add the chicken and stir-fry until cooked and the onion and garlic are lightly browned. Add the courgettes and stir-fry about 1-2 minutes. Add the drained noodles and cook for 2-3 minutes. Add the soy sauce and prawns, season with salt and pepper and cook to heat through. Serve garnished with the spring onions and chilli.

STIR-FRIED GLASS NOODLES WITH CHICKEN

This is a typical Thai stir-fry using cellophane noodles to give a finely textured dish.

Serves 4

INGREDIENTS
1 chicken breast, skinned and boned
2 tbsps oyster sauce
2 tbsps fish sauce
1 tbsp soy sauce
1 tsp palm sugar
½ large red chilli, seeded and chopped
½ tsp grated fresh root ginger
175g/6oz cellophane noodles
2 tbsps oil
2 cloves garlic, crushed
1 red onion, sliced
Coriander leaves, to garnish

Cut the chicken into thin slices. Combine the oyster sauce, fish sauce, soy, sugar, chilli and ginger in a shallow dish. Add the chicken and toss until well coated. Leave to marinate for 20 minutes.

Soak the noodles in boiling water for 5 minutes, until softened. Drain and set aside. Heat the oil in a wok and fry the garlic and onion until just softened. Add the chicken and the marinade and stir-fry for about 10 minutes or until the chicken is cooked through. Add the noodles to the wok and toss over a low heat until heated through. Pile on to a serving dish and garnish with coriander leaves.

CHICKEN AND GRAPE PASTA SALAD

Chicken and grapes complement each other perfectly. Grapes are the classic garnish for Coronation Chicken, on which this recipe is based. It is easiest to use seedless grapes for this recipe.

Serves 4-6

INGREDIENTS

340g/12oz pasta spirals or bows
1-2 tbsps olive oil
1 onion, finely chopped
225g/8oz cooked chicken, shredded
1 red pepper, finely chopped
120g/4oz green grapes, seeded
120g/4oz black grapes, seeded
150ml/¼ pint mayonaise
150ml/¼ pint natural yogurt
1-2 tsps curry paste
Salt and freshly ground black pepper
Freshly chopped coriander, to garnish

Cook the pasta in plenty of boiling, salted water until tender but still firm, about 10-12 minutes. Drain, then rinse in cold water and drain again. Leave until cold.

Heat the olive oil in a small frying pan, add the onion and cook gently for 3-4 minutes until softened. Allow to cool.

Mix together the chicken and pepper. Cut the grapes in half lengthways if they are large and add them to the chicken with the cold cooked pasta and onion. Mix together the mayonnaise and yogurt and add curry paste to taste. Season the salad with salt and pepper then pour the dressing over and toss until the pasta is well coated. Chill until required and garnish with coriander just before serving.

PASTA WITH MEAT

Without doubt the vast majority of pasta recipes, and certainly most of the classic recipes, are Italian in origin. That is, of course, excepting those for noodles and vermicelli that are Chinese! So, many of the recipes that are featured in this chapter on pasta and meat include the most popular ingredients in the Italian cuisine.

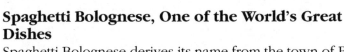

Spaghetti Bolognese, One of the World's Great Dishes

Spaghetti Bolognese derives its name from the town of Bologna in the Emilia-Romagna region of northern Italy. Referred to as *Bologna la grassa*, Bologna the fat, this city is the culinary capital of northern Italy, producing delicious and very rich food from the wealth of top quality ingredients that are produced in the surrounding region. These included Parma ham, Parmesan cheese, and balsamic vinegar.

A Bolognese sauce may be made with minced beef only, or with a mixture of minced beef and pork and some chopped chicken livers. The latter is the more traditional style of the gastronomes of Bologna, as it produces a richer sauce of more complex flavours than a straight beef mixture. The richest of sauces may have a little brandy added to the browned meats but it is far more usual to add some red wine and to reduce that for a strong flavour in the sauce, if some alcohol is required. I always like to add a few mushrooms to a Bolognese – others add peas, carrots or even broccoli florets.

Spaghetti Bolognese must be one of the most popular dishes in the world which, in a sense, is responsible for the move away from the most traditional meat sauce with chicken livers to any one of the numerous recipes that exist, bearing the classic name of Bolognese. When I have my Very Serious Cook's hat on, I get upset about this and feel that it leads to a watering down of an important culinary heritage. However for most of the time, when I am trying to encourage people to enjoy cooking and eating, I feel that as long as there is love in the preparation of a meal and enjoyment in the eating, the actual name of the dish does not really matter.

Game Sauces for Pasta

The Italians are great meat-eaters and, alongside beef, veal, pork and chicken, they also enjoy a wide variety of game. Hare and rabbit are both popular, so it is no surprise to find recipes in this chapter for a hare sauce and a ravioli stuffed with rabbit. I feel that this is good, as such dishes provide different and imaginative ways of serving simple country food. I, for one, would far rather eat a hare sauce on pasta than hare jugged with its blood. It is a great shame that recipes such as the latter can put us off the basic ingredient and prevent us from trying other, delicious dishes.

195

Sweet and Flavoursome Bacon

So often bacon is just regarded as a breakfast food and a seasoning to fry with vegetables at the start of a complicated meat dish. Good bacon is not always easy to find – much of that which is pre-packed seems to be very wet and watery, and to spatter in the pan and never go crisp. Perhaps that limits its use to a *mirepoix*, a mixture of finely diced vegetables and bacon sweated in butter. However, get hold of a good piece of well cured, dry bacon and you have the basis of some wonderful pasta dishes.

What is the difference between bacon and ham? Well, bacon is taken from the back or side of a pig and hams are produced mainly from the back legs and are cured much more slowly than bacon. The shoulder or front leg is also used to produce ham, but this is of a lesser quality than the prime joints from the back leg.

Bacon is usually cured in brine, although a better flavour is produced when it is dry cured. A very mild cure is known as tendersweet, but it produces a very mild bacon. The bacon may then be smoked, adding extra flavour and colour to the meat. Bacon which has not been smoked is referred to as *green*, an unfortunate term as it makes one think of food that has gone off! However, for cooking I certainly prefer to use green bacon as I like the true bacon flavour without the smoke.

Carbonara is probably the most famous pasta sauce with bacon. In the recipe for Tagliatelli Carbonara in this chapter a little paprika is added to the bacon during cooking – I sometimes omit the paprika and add a clove (or two) of crushed garlic.

PASTA AL FORNO

'Al Forno' means baked in the oven, so this is oven-baked pasta.

Serves 4

INGREDIENTS
225g/8oz macaroni
60g/2oz butter or margarine
60g/2oz Parmesan cheese, grated
Pinch of grated nutmeg
Salt and freshly ground black
  pepper
2 eggs, beaten
1 medium onion, chopped
1 clove garlic, crushed
460g/1lb minced beef
2 tbsps tomato purée
6 tbsps beef stock
2 tbsps freshly chopped parsley
4 tbsps red wine
2 tbsps plain flour
150ml/¼ pint milk

Preheat the oven to 190°C/375°F/Mark 5. Cook the macaroni in plenty of boiling salted water for 10 minutes, or until tender but still firm. Rinse under hot water and drain. Place one third of the butter in the pan and return the macaroni to it. Add half the cheese, nutmeg, and salt and pepper to taste and leave to cool. Mix in half the beaten egg, and put aside until required.

Melt half the remaining butter in a pan, and fry the onion and garlic gently until the onion is soft. Increase the heat, add the meat and fry until browned. Add the tomato purée, stock, parsley and wine, and season with salt and pepper. Simmer for 20 minutes. Melt the rest of the butter in a small pan. Stir in the flour and cook for 30 seconds, them remove from the heat and gradually stir in the milk. Bring to the boil, stirring continuously, until the sauce thickens. Beat in the remaining egg and season to taste. Spoon half the macaroni into a serving dish and cover with the meat sauce. Add another layer of macaroni then add the white sauce, top with remaining cheese and bake in the oven for 30 minutes, until golden brown. Serve immediately.

TAGLIATELLE WITH BACON AND TOMATO SAUCE

Serves 4

INGREDIENTS

1 tbsp olive oil
1 onion, finely chopped
6 rashers of bacon, rind
  removed, and cut into strips
2 tbsps freshly chopped parsley
2 tbsps freshly chopped basil
400g/14oz can chopped tomatoes
Salt and freshly ground black
  pepper
280g/10oz tagliatelle
60g/2oz pecorino cheese, grated

Heat the oil in a large pan, add the onion and bacon and cook gently until the onion is soft, but not browned. Add the parsley, basil and tomatoes and simmer gently for 5 minutes, stirring occasionally, then season to taste with salt and pepper.

Meanwhile, cook the tagliatelle in a large pan of boiling salted water. Cook for about 10 minutes, until *al dente*. Drain and return the pasta to the pan. Add the sauce and toss thoroughly. Serve with grated pecorino cheese.

FRIED NOODLES WITH PORK AND VEGETABLES

The boiled noodles need to be well dried before frying to prevent any spatter. Taro is a potato-like vegetable, very similar to edo, which are available in most large supermarkets.

Serves 4

INGREDIENTS

350g/12oz fresh noodles
1 taro or edo
1 tbsp oil
1 clove garlic, chopped
1 carrot, cut into sticks
225g/8oz Chinese leaves, thinly sliced
225g/8oz cooked pork meat, thinly sliced
1 tbsp soy sauce
280ml/½ pint chicken stock
Salt and freshly ground black pepper
Oil for deep-frying
1 tsp cornflour, combined with a little water

Cook the noodles in boiling, salted water, rinse in warm water and set aside to drain. Prepare the taro by first slicing off the end then peeling with a potato peeler. Lastly, using the potato peeler, cut the taro into thin slices. Heat the oil in a wok and stir-fry the taro, garlic, carrot and Chinese leaves. Add the pork, soy sauce, stock and salt and pepper. Cook over a gentle heat for 5 minutes, shaking the wok frequently.

Heat the oil for deep-frying to 180°C/350°F/Mark 4 and fry the noodles a few at a time. Drain the noodles on absorbent kitchen paper. Divide the noodles equally between four small plates. Remove the vegetables and pork mixture from the wok with a slotted spoon and serve over the noodles. Stir the cornflour into the remaining sauce in the wok and stir until the sauce boils and thickens. Pour some over each plate of noodles and serve immediately.

PORK WRAPPED IN NOODLES

This recipe is not as fiddly as it sounds! The meatballs are only mildly spiced and should be served with a hot chilli dipping sauce.

Serves 4

INGREDIENTS
225g/8oz minced pork
1 tsp ground coriander
1 tbsp fish sauce
1 small egg, beaten
90g/3oz rice noodles (vermicelli)
Oil for deep-frying
Whole chillies, to garnish

Mix together the pork, coriander and fish sauce, then add enough egg to bind. Roll the mixture into small balls and chill for 30 minutes. Cover the noodles with warm water and soak for about 10 minutes to soften. Drain the noodles then wrap several strands around each pork ball. Heat the oil in a wok and deep-fry a few of the meatballs at a time for 3-4 minutes or until crisp and golden. Drain on kitchen paper and garnish with whole chillies.

CHAING MAI NOODLES

The coconut milk used in this recipe gives an unusual but typically Thai flavour to this noodle dish.

Serves 4-6

INGREDIENTS

2 tbsps oil
2 cloves garlic, crushed
4 shallots, chopped
1 tbsp red curry paste
½ tsp ground turmeric
Pinch of ground cumin
Pinch of ground coriander
280ml½ pint coconut milk
225g/8oz rump or sirloin steak, thinly sliced
5 tbsps fish sauce
60g/2oz palm sugar
1 tbsp soy sauce
2 tbsps lime juice
1 tbsp freshly chopped garlic chives
460g/1lb fresh egg noodles

Heat the oil in a wok and fry the garlic and shallots until softened. Stir in the curry paste, turmeric, cumin and coriander. Stir-fry for 1 minute. Add the coconut milk and bring to the boil, reduce the heat and add the beef. Simmer for 15-20 minutes or until the beef is cooked. Stir in the fish sauce, sugar, soy, lime juice and garlic chives. Meanwhile, cook the egg noodles in boiling water for 1 minute. Drain and arrange on a serving dish. Spoon the beef on top and serve.

PENNE WITH HAM AND ASPARAGUS

*Penne are pasta tubes, cut diagonally in the shape of a quill.
Penne actually means quill.*

Serves 4

INGREDIENTS
340g/12oz fresh asparagus
30g/1oz butter or margarine
120g/4oz cooked ham
280ml/½ pint double cream
Salt and freshly ground black
   pepper
225g/8oz penne
Parmesan cheese, grated

Using a swivel vegetable peeler, scrape the sides of the asparagus spears starting about 5cm/2 inches from the tips. Cut off the ends of the spears about 2.5cm/1 inch from the bottom. Cut the ham into strips about 1.25cm/½ inch thick. Bring a sauté or frying pan of water to the boil, adding a pinch of salt. Move the pan so it is half on and half off the direct heat. Add the asparagus spears so that the tips are off the heat. Cover the pan and return it to the boil. Cook the asparagus spears for about 2 minutes. Drain and allow to cool. Cut the asparagus into 5cm/2 inch lengths, leaving the tips whole.

Melt the butter in the sauté pan and add the asparagus and ham. Cook briefly to evaporate any liquid, then add the cream. Bring to the boil and cook for about 5 minutes to thicken the cream. Season to taste. Meanwhile, cook the pasta in boiling salted water for about 10-12 minutes. Drain the pasta and rinse under hot water. Toss in a colander to drain then mix with the sauce. Serve with grated Parmesan cheese, if wished.

LAMB WITH PASTA AND TOMATOES

This delicious dish is a classic Greek way of serving lamb, with pasta to make the meat go further.

Serves 6-8

INGREDIENTS

1 leg or shoulder of lamb, about 1.4kg/3lb in weight
2 cloves garlic, cut into thin slivers
4 tbsps olive oil
225g/8oz pasta shells, spirals or other shapes
570ml/1 pint lamb or beef stock or water
460g/1lb fresh tomatoes or 400g/14oz can tomatoes
1 tbsp freshly chopped oregano
Salt and freshly ground black pepper
Parmesan cheese, grated

Preheat the oven to 200°C/400°F/Mark 6. Cut slits at about 5cm/2 inch intervals all over the lamb. Insert small slivers of garlic into each slit. Place the lamb in a large roasting tin and rub the surface with the olive oil. Cook in the preheated oven for about 60 minutes, basting occasionally.

Meanwhile, parboil the pasta for about 5 minutes in boiling salted water and rinse in hot water. Turn the meat over in the roasting tin and add the stock or water, pasta and additional seasoning. Mix the tomatoes with the oregano and salt and pepper and pour over the lamb. Stir well. Cook for an additional 20-30 minutes, stirring the pasta occasionally to ensure even cooking. When the pasta is completely cooked, turn the lamb over again and sprinkle with some cheese before carving and serving with the pasta.

ITALIAN PASTA SALAD

Serve this salad with sliced tomatoes and Italian olive oil bread.

Serves 4-6

INGREDIENTS
460g/1lb pasta shapes
120g/4oz frozen peas
225g/8oz assorted Italiana meats, cut in strips: salami, mortadella, prosciutto, coppa, bresaola
120g/4oz provolone or fontina cheese, cut in strips
15 black olives, halved and pitted
4 tbsps small capers
1 small red onion or 2 shallots, chopped
175g/6oz oyster mushrooms, stems trimmed and sliced

Dressing
3 tbsps white wine vinegar
150ml/¼ pint olive oil
½ clove garlic, minced
1 tsp fennel seeds, crushed
1 tbsp freshly chopped parsley
1 tbsp freshly chopped basil
1 tbsp mustard
Salt and freshly ground black pepper

Cook the pasta in a large pan of boiling salted water for about 10 minutes, or until just tender. Add the frozen peas during the last 3 minutes of cooking time. Drain the pasta and peas and rinse under hot water. Leave in cold water until ready to use.

Mix the dressing ingredients together and drain the pasta and peas. Mix the pasta and peas with the Italian meats and cheeses, olives, capers, chopped onion or shallot and sliced mushrooms. Pour the dressing over the salad and toss all the ingredients together. Do not over-mix. Leave the salad to chill for up to 1 hour before serving.

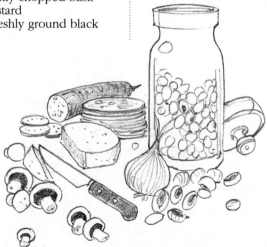

TORTELLINI WITH MUSHROOMS AND BACON

Fresh tortellini are quite time consuming to prepare, but the dried or fresh ones available in supermarkets make a good, quick supper dish when served in a tasty sauce.

Serves 4

INGREDIENTS

175g/6oz streaky bacon, rinded, chopped
1 small onion, chopped
3 tsps cornflour
150ml/¼ pint milk
225g/8oz small button mushrooms
2 tsps ground coriander
280ml/½ pint single cream
Salt and freshly ground black pepper
225g/8oz prepared tortellini, dried or fresh
Freshly chopped coriander leaves

Cook the bacon gently until the fat runs out. Add the onions and cook for 5 minutes until soft. Add the cornflour, cook 2 minutes, then gradually add milk and bring slowly to the boil. Add the mushrooms and cook for a further 2 minutes. Add the ground coriander and cream, and heat through. Season to taste. Cook the tortellini as directed, then fold them into the sauce. Serve garnished with fresh coriander.

LAYERED PASTA SALAD

This layered salad may be prepared the day before it is required – but I prefer to make such dishes on the day.

Serves 4

INGREDIENTS
120g/4oz pasta tubes or spirals
225g/8oz packet frozen peas
1 red onion, thinly sliced
4 radishes, sliced
Crisp lettuce leaves
225g/8oz cooked ham, cut into
  strips
175g/6oz Cheddar cheese, diced
Freshly chopped parsley to
  garnish

Dressing
150ml/¼ pint mayonnaise
150ml/¼ pint soured cream
1 tbsp Dijon or whole grain
  mustard

Cook the pasta in plenty of boiling, salted water until tender, then drain and rinse in cold water, then leave to cool. Cook the frozen peas, drain and cool. Mix together the onion and radishes.

Place the torn lettuce leaves in a large glass bowl. Follow with a layer of the ham, then cheese, half the onion mixture, the pasta, another layer of onion mix, then lastly the peas. Combine the dressing ingredients and spread over the salad. Garnish with chopped parsley.

RABBIT RAVIOLI WITH TARRAGON

This is a well flavoured, country dish. Chicken may be used in place of the rabbit, if preferred.

Serves 4

INGREDIENTS

340g/12oz plain flour
4 eggs, lightly beaten
½ leek
1 onion
1 carrot
3 rabbit thigh portions
2 tbsps olive oil
5 sprigs tarragon
1 bouquet garni
Salt and freshly ground black pepper
4 tbsps double cream

Place the flour in a bowl and add 3 of the eggs. Mix with your fingers to make a dough and form it into a ball. Knead until smooth then set aside to rest. Dice the leek, onion and carrot. Fry the rabbit in the oil until lightly browned. Remove the tarragon leaves from 3 sprigs, reserve the stalks for the stock, and chop the leaves. Add the onion, carrot, leek, tarragon stalks and bouquet garni to the rabbit. Cook for 2 minutes, then add 700ml/¼ pints of water. Cook, covered, over a low heat for 1½ hours, then when cooked, remove the rabbit portions from the pan and take the meat off the bones. Chop it very finely and mix with ¾ of the tarragon leaves, then season with salt and pepper. Strain the stock through a fine sieve and set aside.

Divide the dough into smaller, flat rounds, and pass them through a pasta machine to form thin pasta strips. Cut the pasta into even-sized rectangles to make ravioli. Mix 2 tbsps of the rabbit stock into the meat and tarragon, and place about 1 tsp of the mixture in the centre of each piece of pasta. Brush the edges of the dough with the remaining beaten egg and fold over the filling to make the ravioli. Pinch the edges together with your fingers, then using a pastry cutter, shape into rounds. Cook the ravioli for 5 minutes in plenty of salted boiling water with the last sprig of tarragon. Drain with a slotted spoon.

Reduce 340ml/12fl oz of the rabbit stock by half. Add the cream and remaining tarragon, season to taste and heat through. Serve the ravioli and cream sauce in soup plates. Garnish with the remaining chopped tarragon.

SICILIAN CANNELLONI

Cannelloni should be cooked in quite a small dish, so that the tops become crisp but the rest of the filled pasta remains soft and moist.

Serves 4

INGREDIENTS
16 cannelloni shells
60g/2oz butter
1 shallot, chopped
4 mushrooms, chopped
2 slices ham, chopped
340g/12oz braising beef, minced
Salt and freshly ground black
  pepper
Butter for greasing
10 thin slices mozzarella cheese
120ml/4fl oz chicken stock

Preheat the oven to 200°C/400°F/Mark 6. Cook the cannelloni in salted, boiling water for 5 minutes. Rinse in hot water then set aside to drain. Melt the butter in a saucepan or casserole and cook the shallot, mushrooms, ham and beef for about 10 minutes. Season with salt and pepper and set aside to cool. Once cooled, fill the cannelloni with the mixture and place in a lightly-greased, ovenproof dish. Place the slices of mozzarella over the cannelloni and then pour in the chicken stock.

Cook the cannelloni in a hot oven for 15-25 minutes – the dish should be heated through and the top should be crisp and golden. Serve piping hot.

MEAT RAVIOLI WITH RED PEPPER SAUCE

Red peppers are used to colour the pasta and flavour the sauce for this innovative and unusual dish.

Serves 4

INGREDIENTS
2 red peppers
200g/7oz flour
2 eggs, lightly beaten
200g/7oz minced beef
1 tbsp freshly chopped parsley
½ onion, chopped
Salt and freshly ground black
  pepper
120ml/4fl oz single cream
90g/3oz butter

Place the red peppers in a food processor and blend until liquid. Transfer to a small bowl and set aside, until the pulp rises to the surface. This takes about 30 minutes.

To make the dough, place the flour in a bowl, add 1 egg and 3 tbsps of the red pepper pulp (not the juice). Mix thoroughly and form into a ball. Knead lightly then set the dough aside for 30 minutes. Mix together the meat, parsley and onion and season with salt and pepper. Roll the dough out very thinly, using a pasta machine if available, and cut into small squares. Place a little stuffing on half of the cut squares. Beat the remaining egg and brush the edges of the dough with the egg. Cover with another square of dough and seal the edges by pinching together with your fingers.

Bring a large saucepan of salted water to the boil and cook the ravioli for about 3 minutes – longer if you prefer your pasta well cooked. While the ravioli are cooking, prepare the sauce by heating the cream with 120ml/4fl oz of the red pepper pulp. Bring to the boil and then whisk in the butter. Drain the ravioli. Serve the pasta with the hot cream sauce poured over.

COUNTRYSIDE SAUCE
WITH FRESH PASTA

This is almost a store-cupboard sauce, quick and easy to prepare from basic ingredients.

Serves 4

INGREDIENTS
300g/11oz pasta
1 tbsp olive oil
1 onion, sliced
2 slices ham, cut into small
  pieces
6 basil leaves, chopped
Tomato, seeded and chopped
Salt and freshly ground black
  pepper
60g/2oz butter
2 tbsps grated Parmesan cheese

Cook the pasta in boiling salted water until tender but still firm. Rinse under hot water and set aside to drain. Heat the olive oil in a frying pan and gently cook the onion, ham, basil and tomato for approximately 20 minutes. Season with salt and pepper. Melt the butter in a saucepan and add the pasta, stirring well. Stir in the sauce and serve when the pasta is hot. Top with the grated Parmesan and serve.

WHOLEWHEAT SPAGHETTI WITH PEAS AND BACON

Peas and bacon in plenty of butter make a simple but tasty flavouring for this pasta.

Serves 4

INGREDIENTS
280g/10oz wholewheat spaghetti
340g/12oz shelled peas
1 tsp sugar
90g/3oz butter or margarine
120g/4oz bacon, rinded and
  diced
Salt and freshly ground black
  pepper

Garnish
Freshly chopped parsley

Cook the spaghetti in plenty of boiling salted water for 10 minutes, or until tender but still firm. Meanwhile, cook the peas in boiling water with a pinch of salt and a teaspoon of sugar. Melt the butter in a pan and fry the bacon. When crisp, add the drained peas, and salt and pepper to taste, then pour over the spaghetti. Toss and serve immediately, garnished with chopped parsley if wished.

BRASCIOLE WITH TAGLIATELLE

This is an elegant dish for a dinner party – the veal rolls may be prepared in advance and refrigerated until needed.

Serves 4

INGREDIENTS
4 veal steaks
4 thin slices ham
30g/1oz Parmesan cheese, grated
Salt and freshly ground black
  pepper
30g/1oz butter or margarine
400g/14oz can tomatoes, sieved,
  or passata
225g/8oz tagliatelle

Bat the veal steaks thinly between two sheets of dampened greaseproof paper. Place a slice of ham on the top of each steak and sprinkle each with a tablespoon of the Parmesan cheese and some freshly ground black pepper. Roll up from a short side, like a Swiss roll, tucking the slices in to form neat parcels. Tie gently with string at each end and in the middle. Heat the butter in a pan and add the veal rolls. Cook gently until lightly browned all over. Add the sieved tomatoes, cover and cook for 15 minutes. Meanwhile, cook the tagliatelle in plenty of boiling salted water for 10 minutes, or until tender but still firm. Rinse in hot water and drain.

Remove the string and cut the veal rolls into 2.5cm/1 inch slices. Toss the tagliatelle together with the tomato sauce and top with the veal and grated Parmesan cheese. Serve immediately.

HARE SAUCE WITH WHOLEWHEAT SPAGHETTI

This dish has a strong, gamy flavour and is a good way of using up a small amount of hare meat.

Serves 4

INGREDIENTS
2 tbsps olive oil
225g/8oz boneless hare, cut into small pieces
2 onions, sliced
120g/4oz streaky bacon, rinded and diced
1 clove garlic, crushed
1 tsp freshly chopped oregano
15g/½oz flour
150ml/¼ pint red wine
Salt and freshly ground black pepper
280g/10oz wholewheat spaghetti

Heat the oil in a heavy pan. Lightly brown the hare pieces then remove them with a slotted spoon and set aside. Add the onion, bacon, garlic and oregano to the oil and fry until lightly coloured. Draw the pan off the heat and stir in the flour. Return the pan to the heat and cook for 2 minutes. Remove from the heat again and gradually add the wine. Bring to the boil, stirring continuously. Add the hare, cover the pan and simmer gently for about 1 hour, until the hare is tender. Add salt and pepper to taste. When the sauce is ready, cook the spaghetti in lots of boiling salted water for about 10 minutes, or until tender but still firm. Rinse in hot water and drain. Serve the hare sauce on a bed of the freshly cooked pasta.

SPAGHETTI WITH EGG, BACON AND MUSHROOM

*Spaghetti, eggs and bacon make a classic combination
of ingredients and the mushrooms add extra flavour to
the dish.*

Serves 4

INGREDIENTS

60g/2oz butter or margarine
225g/8oz mushrooms, sliced
120g/4oz bacon, rinded and
  diced
280g/10oz spaghetti
Salt and freshly ground black
  pepper
2 eggs, hard-boiled and finely
  chopped
1 tbsp freshly chopped parsley
60g/2oz Parmesan cheese, grated

Melt half the butter in a frying-pan, add the mushrooms and bacon, and cook for 10 minutes over a moderate heat, until the bacon is crisp. Meanwhile, cook the spaghetti in lots of boiling salted water until tender but still firm – about 10 minutes. Drain and return to the pan. Add the remaining butter, salt and lots of freshly ground black pepper, and the mushrooms and bacon. Toss together. Serve topped with the hard-boiled eggs and parsley. Serve the grated Parmesan cheese separately.

PASTA SPIRALS WITH KIDNEYS IN MARSALA SAUCE

Kidneys are one of my favourite foods – I cook them with plenty of black pepper and serve them on a bed of pasta.

Serves 4

INGREDIENTS
225g/8oz lambs' kidneys
Salt and freshly ground black
  pepper
1 tbsp flour
60g/2oz butter or margarine
1 small onion, finely chopped
1 clove garlic crushed
90g/3oz bacon, rinded and diced
120g/4oz button mushrooms,
  sliced
90ml/3fl oz Marsala, or dry white
  wine
280g/10oz pasta spirals

Remove the skin, fat and hard core from the kidneys. Cut in half lengthways. Add salt and pepper to the flour and mix well, then coat the kidneys in the seasoned flour.

Heat the butter in a pan, add the onion and garlic and cook until soft but not browned. Add the kidneys and brown all over. Add the bacon and mushrooms and cook, stirring frequently, for 3 minutes, then add the Marsala and bring to the boil. Simmer gently for 15 minutes, or until the kidneys are tender. Adjust the seasoning to taste.

Meanwhile, cook the pasta spirals in plenty of boiling salted water for 10 minutes, or until tender but still firm. Rinse in hot water and drain well. Serve the kidneys on a bed of the freshly cooked pasta.

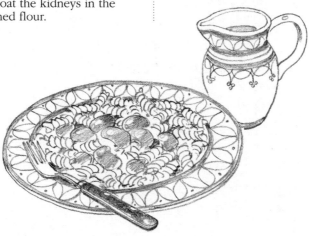

SPAGHETTI WITH SWEETBREAD CARBONARA

Sweetbreads are used in place of bacon for this variation of a popular classic. Stir the eggs into the spaghetti over a low heat until they just start to thicken, if necessary.

Serves 4

INGREDIENTS
1 onion, chopped
3 tbsps olive oil
340g/12oz wholewheat spaghetti
225g/8oz calves' sweetbreads, blanched, skinned and chopped
6 tbsps dry white wine
4 eggs, lightly beaten
60g/2oz Parmesan cheese, grated
2 tbsps freshly chopped basil
1 clove garlic, crushed
Salt and freshly ground black pepper
Fresh basil, to garnish

Fry the onion gently in the olive oil for 5 minutes. Meanwhile, cook the spaghetti in a large pan of boiling, salted water for about 10 minutes, until just tender. Add the chopped sweetbreads to the onion and fry gently for 4 minutes, then add the white wine and cook briskly until it has almost evaporated. Beat the eggs with the Parmesan cheese, basil, garlic and salt and pepper. Drain the spaghetti thoroughly; immediately stir in the beaten egg mixture and the sweetbreads so that the heat from the spaghetti cooks the eggs. Garnish with basil and serve immediately.

TAGLIATELLE CARBONARA

This dish is often made with spaghetti but tagliatelle is my favourite.

Serves 2

INGREDIENTS
1 tbsp olive oil
120g/4oz streaky bacon, rinded
  and chopped
Pinch of paprika
4 tbsps single cream
2 eggs, lightly beaten
60g/2oz Parmesan cheese, grated
280g/10oz tagliatelle
30g/1oz butter or margarine
Salt and freshly ground black
  pepper

Heat the oil in a frying pan, add the bacon and cook over a moderate heat until browned. Add the paprika and cook for 1 minute, then add the cream and stir. Beat together the eggs and grated cheese.

Meanwhile, cook the tagliatelle in lots of boiling salted water for 10 minutes, or until tender but still firm. Drain then return to the pan with the butter and black pepper, and toss. Add the bacon mixture and the egg mixture, and toss together over a low heat until the egg is just setting. Add salt to taste. Serve immediately.

PENNE WITH SPICY CHILLI SAUCE

Penne are slightly thicker than macaroni – I like them because more sauce gets trapped inside the tubes!

Serves 4-6

INGREDIENTS
400g/14oz can plum tomatoes
1 tbsp olive oil
2 cloves garlic, crushed
1 onion, chopped
4 rashers of bacon, chopped
2 red chillies, seeded and
  chopped
2 spring onions, chopped
60g/2oz pecorino or Parmesan
  cheese, grated
460g/1lb penne or macaroni
Salt and freshly ground black
  pepper

Chop the tomatoes and sieve them to remove the pips. Alternatively, use a can of chopped tomatoes. Heat the oil in a frying pan and fry the garlic, onion and bacon gently for 6-8 minutes. Add the sieved tomatoes, chillies, spring onions and half the cheese. Simmer gently for 20 minutes then season to taste.

Cook the penne or macaroni in boiling salted water for 10-15 minutes, or until tender. Rinse under hot water and drain well. Place the cooked penne in a warm serving dish with half the sauce and toss them together to coat the pasta. Pour the remaining sauce over the top and sprinkle with the remaining cheese before serving.

MEE GORENG

I love Indonesian food, which is spicy and hot. This dish of mixed noodles is quick to prepare but have everything chopped before you start cooking. Use chilli sauce if chilli paste is not available.

Serves 4

INGREDIENTS
225g/8oz fine egg noodles
4 tbsps peanut oil
1 onion, finely chopped
2 cloves garlic, crushed
1 green chilli, seeded and finely
  sliced
1 tsp chilli paste
120g/4oz pork fillet or
  tenderloin, finely sliced
2 sticks of celery, sliced
¼ small cabbage, finely shredded
1 tbsp light soy sauce
120g/4oz cooked prawns, shelled
  and deveined
Salt and freshly ground black
  pepper

Soak the noodles in hot water for 8 minutes, until they are soft. Rinse in cold water and drain thoroughly in a colander.

Heat the oil in a wok and stir-fry the onion, garlic and chilli until the onion is soft and just golden brown. Add the chilli paste and stir well, then add the pork, celery and cabbage to the fried onions, and stir-fry for about 3 minutes, or until the pork is cooked through. Season to taste. Stir in the soy sauce, noodles and prawns, tossing the mixture together and heating through before serving.

MACARONI AU GRATIN

This is a typical Mediterranean dish, and a very good way of turning just a little meat into a satisfying meal for four.

Serves 4

INGREDIENTS
460g/1lb macaroni
60g/2oz butter
Salt and freshly ground black
  pepper
120g/4oz Parmesan cheese,
  grated
250g/9oz lamb, minced
3 tbsps breadcrumbs

Preheat the oven to 200°C/400°F/Gas Mark 6. Cook the macaroni in boiling, salted water. Drain and rinse, then set aside to drain. Melt the butter and fry the macaroni rapidly, seasoning it with salt and pepper. Place a layer of macaroni in the bottom of a greased ovenproof dish and then a layer of cheese. Sprinkle the meat over the cheese and then cover the meat with another layer of macaroni. Sprinkle over another layer of cheese and then all the breadcrumbs. Bake in a hot oven for 20 to 30 minutes and serve immediately.

PHARAOH'S WHEEL
NOODLES

This recipe is based on a traditional Jewish dish said to symbolise the Jews crossing of the Red Sea. I prefer to use tomato sauce, rather than the meat sauce and allow the salami to flavour the dish.

Serves 6

INGREDIENTS
225g/8oz egg noodles, cooked until *al dente*
420ml/¾ pint Italian meat sauce or tomato sauce
225g/8oz salami, thinly sliced
60g/2oz raisins
60g/2oz pine nuts

Preheat the oven to 200°C/ 400°F/Gas Mark 6. Grease a large ovenproof round, glass baking dish. Arrange a layer of cooked noodles in the dish, then pour some of the sauce over them. Arrange a ring of salami round the edge of the dish and sprinkle some raisins and pine nuts in the centre. Add another layer of pasta and repeat the sauce, salami, raisins and pine nuts. Continue layering until all the ingredients are used up, finishing with a layer of salami. Bake for 20 minutes, or until heated through. Serve immediately.

SPAGHETTI WITH TOMATO, SALAMI AND GREEN OLIVES

Salami is usually eaten cold but it makes a really tasty addition to hot pasta dishes.

Serves 3-4

INGREDIENTS
400g/14oz can plum tomatoes or passata
2 tsps freshly chopped oregano
150g/5oz salami, sliced and shredded
200g/7oz green olives, pitted and chopped
Salt and freshly ground black pepper
280g/10oz spaghetti
2 tbsps olive oil
1 clove garlic, crushed
60g/2oz pecorino cheese, grated

Purée the tomatoes in a liquidiser or food processor, then push through a sieve into a saucepan. Alternatively use passata. Add the oregano, salami and olives, and heat gently. Add salt and pepper to taste.

Meanwhile, cook the spaghetti in plenty of boiling, salted water for 10 minutes, or until tender but still firm. Drain well. Heat the olive oil and add the garlic and some freshly ground black pepper to the pan used to cook the spaghetti. Return the spaghetti to the pan, and add the sauce. Toss well. Serve immediately topped with the pecorino cheese.

FARFALLE WITH BEEF, MUSHROOM AND SOURED CREAM

This is a luxurious dish using a prime cut of steak but, mixed with the pasta, a little beef goes a long way.

Serves 2-3

INGREDIENTS

225g/8oz fillet or rump steak, sliced
30g/1oz unsalted butter
1 onion, sliced
120g/4oz mushrooms, sliced
1 tbsp flour
4 tbsps soured cream
10 green olives, pitted and chopped
Salt and freshly ground black pepper
280g/10oz farfalle (pasta bows)

Garnish
Soured cream
1 tbsp freshly chopped parsley

Cut the meat into small, thin slices with a sharp knife. Heat half the butter and fry the meat over a high heat until well browned. Remove the meat with a draining spoon and set aside. Heat the remaining butter in the pan, and gently fry the onion until soft and just beginning to colour. Add the mushrooms and cook for 3 minutes, then stir in the flour and continue frying for a further 3 minutes. Gradually stir in the soured cream, then add the meat, olives, and salt and pepper to taste.

Meanwhile, cook the farfalle in plenty of boiling, salted water for 10 minutes, or until tender but still firm. Drain well. Serve the pasta with the beef and mushroom sauce on top. Garnish with a little extra soured cream and chopped parsley.

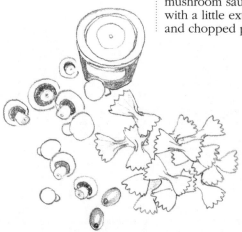

ITALIAN CASSEROLE

*Macaroni is used to thicken a savoury sauce in this recipe,
turning it into a filling, family casserole.*

Serves 4

INGREDIENTS
90g/3oz small macaroni
60g/2oz butter or margarine
1 onion, chopped
1 clove garlic, crushed
2 × 400g/14oz can plum
  tomatoes
1 tbsp tomato purée
1 red pepper, roughly chopped
1 green pepper, roughly
  chopped
225g/8oz salami, cut into chunks
10 black olives, halved, and
  pitted
Salt and freshly ground black
  pepper
120g/4oz mozzarella cheese,
  thinly sliced

Preheat the oven to
180°C/350°F/Mark 4. Cook the
macaroni in plenty of boiling,
salted water for 10 minutes, or
until tender but still firm. Rinse
under hot water and drain well,
then place in a shallow,
ovenproof dish.

Meanwhile, heat the butter in a
pan and fry the onion and garlic
gently until soft. Add the
undrained tomatoes, tomato
purée, red and green peppers,
salami and olives, and stir well.
Simmer, uncovered, for 5
minutes, then season with salt
and pepper to taste. Pour the
sauce over the macaroni, stir, and
cover with the sliced cheese.
Bake uncovered in the preheated
oven for 20 minutes, until the
cheese has melted. Serve
immediately.

TAGLIATELLE WITH
CREAMY LIVER SAUCE

I love chicken livers, especially in a creamy sauce with pasta.

Serves 4

INGREDIENTS
2 medium onions, sliced
1 clove garlic, crushed
4 tbsps olive oil
120g/4oz mushrooms, sliced
460g/1lb chicken livers, cleaned
  and sliced
120ml/4fl oz single cream
2 eggs, beaten
Salt and freshly ground black
  pepper
280g/10oz tagliatelle
Olive oil
1 tbsp freshly chopped parsley

In a large frying pan, cook the onions and garlic gently in the oil until softened. Add the mushrooms and cook for 3 minutes. Add the chicken livers to the onions and mushrooms, and cook until lightly browned. Remove the pan from the heat and stir in the cream. Return to a low heat and cook, uncovered, for a further 2 minutes. Remove from the heat, and stir in the lightly beaten eggs. Season with salt and pepper to taste.

Meanwhile, cook the tagliatelle in plenty of boiling salted water for 10 minutes, or until tender but still firm, stirring occasionally. Drain the tagliatelle, toss in a little olive oil and black pepper. Serve the sauce over the tagliatelle and sprinkle with the parsley.

PASTITSIO

This is a hearty bake, very similar to a traditional Maltese dish which is actually topped with a pastry crust.

Serves 4

INGREDIENTS
225g/8oz macaroni
90g/3oz butter or margarine
60g/2oz Parmesan cheese, grated
Pinch of grated nutmeg
Salt and freshly ground black
    pepper
2 eggs, beaten
1 medium onion, chopped
1 clove garlic, crushed
460g/1lb minced beef
2 tbsps tomato purée
90ml/3fl oz beef stock
2 tbsps freshly chopped parsley
4 tbsps red wine
30g/1oz plain flour
280ml/½ pint milk

Preheat the oven to 190°C/375°F/Mark 5. Cook the macaroni in plenty of boiling, salted water for 10 minutes, or until tender but still firm. Rinse under hot water and drain. Place one-third of the butter in the pan and return the macaroni to it. Add half the cheese, the nutmeg and salt and pepper to taste. Leave to cool slightly then mix in half the beaten egg, and set aside.

Melt half of the remaining butter in a pan, and fry the onion and garlic gently until the onion is soft. Increase the heat, add the meat, and fry until browned. Add the tomato purée, stock, parsley and wine, and season with salt and pepper. Simmer for 20 minutes.

In a small pan, melt the rest of the butter, then stir in the flour and cook for 30 seconds. Remove from the heat, and stir in the milk. Bring to the boil, stirring continuously, until the sauce thickens. Beat in the remaining egg and season to taste. Spoon half the macaroni into a serving dish and cover with the meat sauce. Add another layer of macaroni. Pour white sauce over the macaroni, sprinkle with the remaining cheese, and bake in the preheated oven for 30 minutes until golden brown. Serve immediately.

MACARONI CHEESE WITH FRANKFURTERS

Macaroni cheese is one of my favourite supper dishes – with frankfurters it is very filling. Brown the dish under a hot grill before serving, if preferred.

Serves 4

INGREDIENTS
8 frankfurters
460g/1lb macaroni
60g/2oz butter or margarine
60g/2oz plain flour
570ml/1 pint milk
175g/6oz Cheddar cheese, grated
1 tsp mustard powder
Salt and freshly ground black
  pepper

Poach the frankfurters for 5-6 minutes in slightly salted boiling water. Skin the frankfurters if preferred and slice the sausages diagonally.

Cook the macaroni in plenty of boiling, salted water for about 20 minutes, or until tender. Rinse in cold water and drain well. Melt the butter in a saucepan, stir in the flour and cook for 1 minute. Remove the pan from the heat and add the milk gradually, beating thoroughly. Return the pan to the heat, bring to the boil, stirring continuously, then simmer for 2 minutes. Stir in the macaroni, frankfurters, grated cheese and mustard. Season to taste and serve.

PORK & PRAWN CHOW MEIN

Chow Mein is a noodle dish, flavoured with small amounts of meat or fish and vegetables.

Serves 4-6

INGREDIENTS
225g/8oz medium dried Chinese
  noodles
2 tbsps oil
225g/8oz pork filled, thinly sliced
1 carrot, shredded
1 small red pepper, thinly sliced
90g/3oz bean sprouts
60g/2oz mangetout
1 tbsp rice wine or dry sherry
2 tbsps soy sauce
120g/4oz peeled, cooked prawns

Cook the noodles in plenty of boiling salted water for about 4-5 minutes. Rinse under hot water and drain thoroughly.

Heat a wok and add the oil. Stir-fry the pork for 4-5 minutes or until almost cooked. Add the carrots to the wok and cook for 1-2 minutes. Add the remaining vegetables, wine and soy sauce. Cook for about 2 minutes. Add the drained noodles and prawns and toss over the heat for 1-2 minutes. Serve immediately.

SPAGHETTI BOLOGNESE

This must surely be one of the most famous dishes in the world – it is certainly one of the most copied and abused! I hope you like this version.

Serves 4

INGREDIENTS
30g/1oz butter or margarine
1 tbsp olive oil
2 onions, finely chopped
1 carrot, diced
225g/8oz minced beef
120g/4oz can tomato purée
Salt and freshly ground black
  pepper
280ml/½ pint brown beef stock
2 tbsps sherry
280g/10oz spaghetti
Parmesan cheese

Heat the butter and oil in a pan and cook the onions and carrot slowly until soft. Increase the heat and add the minced beef. Fry for a few minutes, then stir, and continue cooking until the meat is browned all over. Add the tomato purée, salt and pepper and the stock. Simmer gently for about 45 minutes, stirring occasionally, until the mixture thickens. Add the sherry to the sauce and cook for a further 5 minutes. Meanwhile, bring a large pan of salted water to the boil, add the spaghetti and cook for 10 minutes, or until *al dente*. Drain. Serve the spaghetti with the Bolognese sauce and grated Parmesan cheese.

FRIED NOODLES WITH PORK AND PRAWNS

Sambal ulek is a spicy Thai relish, used much as we would use chutney. When added to dishes during cooking, it gives a rich, hot flavour.

Serves 4

INGREDIENTS

225g/8oz Chinese noodles
4 tbsps oil
1 onion, finely chopped
2 cloves garlic, crushed
1 green chilli, seeded and sliced
1 tsp sambal ulek
120g/4oz pork, finely sliced
2 sticks celery, shredded
¼ head of Chinese leaves, shredded
1 tbsp light soy sauce
120g/4oz prawns shelled and de-veined
Salt and freshly ground black pepper

Garnish
Sliced cucumber
Sliced spring onions

Soak the noodles in hot water for 8 minutes, or boil until cooked. Rinse in hot water then leave them to drain in a colander.

Heat a wok or large frying pan and add the oil. Stir-fry the onion, garlic and chilli until the onion begins to colour. Add the sambal ulek, pork, celery, Chinese leaves and a pinch of salt and pepper. Stir-fry for 3 minutes. Add the soy sauce, drained noodles and prawns and toss the mixture to heat through well. Place in a warmed serving dish, surround with sliced cucumber and sprinkle the onions on top.

SPICY STEAMED PORK WITH NOODLES

The combination of spicy meatballs, bok choy or spinach, noodles and fresh coriander makes a simple but memorable dish.

Serves 4

INGREDIENTS

225g/8oz minced pork
1 tsp ground coriander
1 tsp ground cumin
1 tsp ground turmeric
1 bunch bok choy or spinach, washed
1-2 tbsps red or green curry paste
1 tsp shrimp paste
150ml/¼ pint thick coconut milk
175g/6oz egg noodles
Freshly chopped coriander, to garnish

Place the minced pork and ground spices in a food processor and process until very finely chopped. Shape the pork mixture into small balls using dampened hands. Tear the bok choy into large pieces and place in a heat-proof dish that will fit into a steamer. Arrange the meat balls on top. Mix together the curry paste, shrimp paste and coconut milk and pour over the meat balls. Cover and steam for 20 minutes. Meanwhile, cook the noodles as directed on the packet. Drain well then mix the noodles together with the pork and bok choy. Garnish with a sprinkling of chopped coriander leaves.

CANNELLONI

Cannelloni should be cooked in a very hot oven to crisp the top of the pasta, whilst leaving most of the dish tender and moist.

Serves 4

INGREDIENTS
Filling
1 tbsp olive oil
2 cloves garlic, crushed
1 onion, chopped
460g/1lb minced beef
1 tsp tomato purée
1 tbsp freshly chopped basil
1 tbsp freshly chopped oregano
225g/8oz frozen spinach, thawed
1 egg, lightly beaten
4 tbsps double cream
Salt and freshly ground black
    pepper

12 cannelloni tubes
2 tbsps Parmesan cheese, grated

Tomato sauce
1 tbsp olive oil
1 onion, chopped
1 clove garlic, crushed
400g/14oz can chopped tomatoes
2 tbsps tomato purée
Salt and freshly ground black
    pepper

Béchamel sauce
280ml/½ pint milk
1 slice of onion
3 peppercorns
1 small bay leaf
30g/1oz butter or margarine
30g/1oz flour
Salt and freshly ground black
    pepper

Prepare the filling. Heat the oil in a pan, and fry the garlic and onion gently until soft and transparent. Add the beef and cook, stirring continuously, until well browned. Drain off any fat, add the tomato purée, basil and oregano, and cook gently for 15 minutes. Add the spinach, egg and cream, and salt and pepper to taste.

Cook the cannelloni in a large pan of boiling, salted water for 15-20 minutes, until tender. Rinse in hot water and drain. Carefully fill the tubes with the meat mixture, using a piping bag with a wide, plain nozzle, or a teaspoon.

Preheat the oven to 230°C/450°F/Gas Mark 8. Make the tomato sauce. Heat the oil in a pan, add the onion and garlic, and cook gently until transparent. Press the tomatoes through a sieve, and add to the pan with the tomato purée, salt and pepper. Bring to the boil, and then simmer for 5 minutes. Set to one side.

To make the béchamel sauce, place the milk in a pan with the onion, peppercorns and bay leaf. Heat gently for 1 minute, taking care not to boil, and set aside to cool for 5 minutes. Strain. Melt the butter in a pan. Remove it from the heat and stir in the flour then gradually add the milk. Bring to the boil, stirring continuously, until the sauce boils and thickens. Season to taste.

Spread the tomato sauce in the base of an ovenproof dish. Lay the cannelloni on top and cover with the béchamel sauce. Sprinkle with the grated cheese, and bake for 10-15 minutes. Serve immediately.

MEAT RAVIOLI

Ravioli are little parcels of pasta traditionally with a meat filling. Homemade ravioli bears little resemblance to the rather non-descript ravioli sold in cans – do try this recipe.

Serves 4

INGREDIENTS
Filling
60g/2oz butter or margarine
1 clove garlic, crushed
1 onion, grated
225g/8oz minced beef
5 tbsps red wine
Salt and freshly ground black
  pepper
2 tbsps breadcrumbs
120g/4oz cooked spinach,
  chopped
2 eggs, beaten

Dough
250g/9oz strong plain flour
3 eggs, lightly beaten

Sauce
400g/14oz can chopped tomatoes
1 small onion, grated
1 small carrot, finely diced
1 bay leaf
2 parsley stalks
Salt and freshly ground black
  pepper
60g/2oz Parmesan cheese

Prepare the filling. Heat the butter in a pan, add the garlic and onion, and fry gently for 1 minute. Add the minced beef, and fry until browned, add the red wine, salt and pepper and cook, uncovered, for 15 minutes. Strain the juices and reserve them for the sauce. Allow the filling to cool then add the breadcrumbs, chopped spinach, and beaten eggs to bind. Add salt and pepper to taste.

To make the dough, sieve the flour into a bowl. Make a well in the centre and add the eggs. Work the flour and eggs together with a fork then knead by hand, until a smooth dough is formed. Wrap the dough in plastic film and leave to rest for 15 minutes in a cool place. Lightly flour a board, and roll the dough out thinly into a rectangle. Cut the dough in half.

Place small piles of the filling about 4cm/1½ inches apart on one half of the dough. Place the remaining dough on top and cut with a ravioli cutter or small pastry cutter. Seal the edges by pinching together.

Cook the ravioli in batches in a large, wide pan with plenty of boiling, salted water until tender – about 8 minutes. Remove the ravioli carefully with a slotted spoon.

To make the sauce, place all the ingredients in a saucepan. Add the reserved juice from the cooked meat, and bring to the boil. Simmer for 10 minutes. Press the sauce through a sieve, and return the smooth sauce to the pan. Adjust the seasoning. Place the ravioli in a warmed serving dish and cover with the tomato sauce. Serve immediately with grated Parmesan cheese.

LASAGNE

Lasagne, a glorious dish of layered pasta, meat sauce and fragrant white sauce, is best made with fresh pasta. If using dried, chose a lasagne which requires pre-cooking – it only takes a few minutes and the flavour is so much better than the no-cook variety.

Serves 4

INGREDIENTS
8 sheets lasagne

Meat sauce
60g/2oz butter or margarine
1 onion, chopped
1 stick celery, sliced
2 carrot, diced
120g/4oz minced beef
1 tbsp flour
1 tbsp tomato purée
150ml/¼ pint beef stock
1 tsp freshly chopped marjoram
Salt and freshly ground black
   pepper

Béchamel sauce
280ml/½ pint milk
6 black peppercorns
Slice of onion
1 bay leaf
Parsley stalks
60g/2oz butter or margarine
45g/1½oz flour

Prepare the meat sauce. Heat the butter in a pan and add the onion, celery and carrot, cook until the onion is golden. Add the minced beef and brown well, then stir in the flour, add the tomato purée, beef stock, marjoram and salt and pepper. Simmer for 15 minutes.

Meanwhile, cook the lasagne in plenty of boiling salted water for 10 minutes, or until tender. Rinse in cold water and drain carefully. Lay the lasagne out on a clean cloth to dry.

Prepare the béchamel sauce. Bring the milk almost to the boil in a saucepan with the peppercorns, onion, bay leaf and parsley stalks and remove from the heat. Allow to cool for 5 minutes, then strain through a sieve to remove the flavourings. Melt the butter in a saucepan, then stir in the flour and cook for 30 seconds. Remove the pan from the heat and gradually add the milk, stirring continuously. Bring to the boil, then simmer for 3 minutes.

Grease an ovenproof baking dish. Line the base with a layer of lasagne. Cover with a layer of meat sauce then a layer of béchamel sauce. Add another layer of lasagne, repeating the layers until all the ingredients are used, finishing with a layer of béchamel sauce. Bake in the preheated oven for about 20 minutes, or until the top is golden. Serve immediately.

SWEET PASTA PUDDINGS

Not all pasta dishes have to be savoury! There are many sweet dishes, usually made with macaroni or one of the other, smaller pasta shapes, that are delicious, especially to serve after a light main course to satisfy a hearty appetite. Pasta puddings are also useful dishes for those who have lost their appetite and are unwell, as a few spoonfuls of a milky pudding will introduce both protein and carbohydrate, as well as a little fat, to the sickroom menu.

Pasta & Fruit

Just as pasta and vegetables provide so many winning combinations of flavours for savoury dishes, so pasta and fruits provide a versatile selection of basic dishes for desserts. I shall not pretend that they are ever likely to be the most sophisticated of dishes, but they are good, honest fare suitable for family meals and informal entertaining.

Many fruits go well with pasta and their seasonal availability suggests whether the dish should be hot or cold. For example, summer fruits such as peaches and strawberries make surprise bases for brulées, the fruit hidden away in the bottom of a dish under a thick layer of creamy pasta and then topped with caramelised sugar and served chilled. I like to cook apricots, plums and damsons to a thick purée and then to serve that swirled into a dish of sweet pasta. A recipe for Creamy Macaroni with Apricot Purée is included in this chapter.

Successful Sweet Pasta Puddings

Puddings are best made with small or thin pastas. When I was a child my mother used to buy thin macaroni for puddings, but this is not so widely available now, so the short-cut, quick-cook macaroni may be used, or vermicelli. Small pastini, the pasta shapes for soup, are also excellent for dessert dishes.

I find that a sweet pasta mix is far more likely to boil over during cooking than a rice pudding, so I cook the pasta in a large pan on the hob, where I can keep an eye on it. Choose a pan that will allow plenty of room for the pasta to cook without sticking together, and will allow the milk to simmer without boiling over. Once the pasta is tender the mixture may be transferred to an ovenproof dish and baked to produce a crisp top, as for a traditional rice pudding.

Vermicelli are really best cooked in boiling water, before being added to other ingredients after cooking, as in the recipe for Honey Vermicelli. If the vermicelli are not boiled quickly enough they will stick together in a solid mass, and it is difficult to keep a pan of milk boiling sufficiently quickly to prevent that from happening, without the milk boiling over.

A Pasta Pudding for a Sophisticated Meal

I have said before that pasta puddings are good, honest, family fare. Well, I have included one recipe here which is an exception to the rule, a sweet ravioli in a soured cream sauce. If you are an experienced ravioli maker, you will think nothing of producing this sweet version of a favourite stuffed pasta. However, non-experienced ravioli makers should not be daunted or discouraged from making this dish. It is actually a very good recipe for entertaining as the ravioli may be made in advance, as may the cherry sauce and cream mixture, and then the sauce may just be reheated while the ravioli is cooking.

The cherry ravioli is best made with fresh, tart black cherries but these are not always easy to obtain so, for ease of shopping, the recipe calls for canned cherries. Do make certain that the cherries are very well drained before they are placed in the ravioli. If they are too moist they will not only make the pasta sticky, but will make it difficult to handle, clinging to the work surface during shaping. Once the ravioli are completed, if they are not to be cooked immediately, I would transfer them to a lightly floured, clean tea-towel to dry – do not leave them on the work surface where they have been made or they will stick.

The Ninth Jewel in Eight Treasure Pudding

The Chinese are not big pudding eaters except at banquets, when their most famous rice pudding, Eight Jewel or Eight Treasure Pudding is served. This is served either as a moulded pudding, filled with a variety of fruits, or as a creamy rice pudding with the fruits mixed into it. I have adapted a recipe for the latter to be made with thin macaroni.

BLACK CHERRY RAVIOLI WITH SOURED CREAM SAUCE

Ravioli may be savoury or sweet – these are filled with tart black cherries.

Serves 4

INGREDIENTS
Dough
250g/9oz strong plain flour
1 tbsp sugar
3 eggs, lightly beaten

460g/1lb can black cherries, pitted
1 tsp arrowroot
60g/2oz granulated sugar
120ml/4fl oz soured cream
120ml/4fl oz double cream

Turn the cherries into a sieve. Strain off and reserve the juice.

Make the dough by sifting the flour and sugar into a bowl. Make a well in the centre and add the lightly-beaten eggs. Work the flour and eggs together with a spoon, and then by hand, until a smooth dough is formed. Knead gently until smooth and shiny. Lightly flour a board, and roll the dough out thinly into a rectangle. Cut the dough in half. Place the well-drained cherries about 4cm/1½ inches apart on the dough. Place the other half on top, and cut with a small glass or pastry cutter. Seal well around the edges with the back of a fork.

Boil plenty of water in a large saucepan, then drop in the cherry pasta. Cook for about 10 minutes, or until they rise to the surface. Remove with a draining spoon and keep warm. Reserve 2 tablespoons of the cherry juice. Mix 1 tablespoon with the arrowroot. Mix any remaining juice with the sugar and set over a medium heat. Add the arrowroot mixture, and heat until it boils and thickens. Meanwhile, mix the soured cream and double cream together and marble the remaining 1 tablespoon of cherry juice through it. Pour the hot, thickened cherry juice over the cherry ravioli. Serve hot, with the cream sauce.

240

HONEY VERMICELLI

Honey, sesame and cinnamon give a Greek flavour to this pasta dessert.

Serves 4

INGREDIENTS
225g/8oz vermicelli
60g/2oz butter
2 tsps sesame seeds
3 tbsps clear honey
¼ tsp cinnamon

Sauce
5 tbsps double cream
5 tbsps soured cream

Cook the vermicelli in boiling water for 5 minutes or until tender, stirring regularly with a fork to separate the noodles. Drain, and spread out to dry on a wire tray covered with absorbent kitchen paper, or a tea-towel. Leave for about an hour.

Make the sauce by mixing the soured cream and double cream together. Melt the butter in a frying pan. Add the sesame seeds, and fry until lightly browned. Stir in the honey, cinnamon and vermicelli, and heat gently. Serve hot, topped with the cream sauce.

CHOCOLATE CREAM HÉLÈNE

Pears and chocolate are a classic combination – with a pasta cream the pudding is a little more substantial.

Serves 4

INGREDIENTS
90g/3oz small pasta shapes for soup
430ml/¾ pint milk
45g/1½oz caster sugar
1 tsp cocoa
1 tbsp hot water
150ml/¼ pint cream, lightly whipped
425g/15oz can pear halves

Decoration
Chocolate, grated

Cook the pasta in the milk and sugar until soft. Stir frequently being careful not to allow the milk to boil over. Meanwhile, dissolve the cocoa in hot water, then stir it into the pasta. Pour the pasta into a bowl to cool. When cool, fold in the lightly whipped cream, then chill. Serve the pasta cream with the pear halves, and a sprinkling of grated chocolate.

CREAM CHEESE MARGHERITA

I usually think of a margherita as a drink or a pizza! Here it's a delicious pasta pudding.

Serves 4

INGREDIENTS
60g/2oz sultanas
Grated rind and juice of half a lemon
120g/4oz small pasta shapes for soup
225g/8oz cream cheese
60g/2oz caster sugar
150ml/¼ pint single cream
½ tsp ground cinnamon

Decoration
1 tbsp flaked almonds
Lemon peel, cut into slivers

Soak the sultanas in the lemon juice for about 1 hour. Meanwhile, cook the pasta in plenty of boiling water until tender, stirring occasionally. Drain and cool. Beat the cream cheese, sugar and cream together until smooth, then beat in the grated lemon rind and cinnamon. Fold in the pasta and sultanas. Divide between individual dessert glasses or small sweet dishes, then cover the tops with flaked almonds and slivers of lemon peel. Chill before serving.

VANILLA CREAM MELBA

Sweet pasta puddings make substantial desserts to serve after a light main course of salad.

Serves 4

INGREDIENTS
90g/3oz small pasta shapes for soup
430ml/¾ pint milk
45g/1½oz brown sugar
Few drops of vanilla essence
150ml/¼ pint cream, lightly whipped
425g/15oz can peach halves
1 tsp cinnamon (optional)

Melba sauce
225g/8oz raspberries
30g/1oz icing sugar

Cook the pasta in the milk and sugar until soft. Stir frequently, being careful not to allow the milk to boil over. Draw off the heat and stir in the vanilla essence. Pour the pasta into a bowl to cool. When cool, fold in the cream and chill.

Meanwhile, make the Melba sauce. Push the raspberries through a sieve, then mix in icing sugar to the desired thickness and taste. Serve the pasta with the peach halves and Melba sauce. Dust with cinnamon if required.

SPAGHETTI DOLCE

This is a very simple pasta, a nursery pudding for big children! I leave the spaghetti in long strands – the sauce is so delicious to suck up with the pasta.

Serves 4

INGREDIENTS
175g/6oz spaghetti
150ml/¼ pint double cream
2 tbsps brandy
Caster sugar to taste

Cook the spaghetti in plenty of boiling water until just tender but still firm. Drain and rinse in boiling water, then drain again and place the spaghetti in a warm serving dish. Mix together the cream, brandy and sugar and pour over the hot spaghetti. Toss, then serve immediately.

EIGHT TREASURE MACARONI

This is a variation on the classic Chinese dessert of Eight Treasure Rice. I find the pudding slightly less rich when made with macaroni.

Serves 4

INGREDIENTS
175g/6oz macaroni
280ml/½ pint double cream
225g/8oz sweetened chestnut
  purée
15 dried red dates
2 tbsps large raisins
60g/2oz walnut halves
30g/1oz almonds
60g/2oz glacé cherries, halved
30g/1oz angelica, chopped
60g/2oz glacé papaya or mango,
  chopped

Cook the macaroni in plenty of boiling water until just tender but still firm. Drain, rinse in boiling water, then drain again. Return the macaroni to the saucepan and stir in the cream and chestnut purée. Heat gently until the chestnut purée has melted into the macaroni.

Roughly chop the dates, raisins and nuts, then add them to the warm macaroni with the remaining ingredients. Stir carefully, then serve the pudding warm.

PEACH BRULÉE

The combination of peaches and creamy macaroni make this a real brulée surprise.

Serves 4

INGREDIENTS
120g/4oz small pasta shapes for soup
2 large, ripe peaches
200ml/7fl oz double cream, lightly whipped
60g/2oz caster sugar
Demerara sugar

Cook the pasta in plenty of boiling water for about 5 minutes, until just tender but still firm. Drain, rinse in cold water and then drain again. Cut the peaches in half and remove the skin and stones. Fan one half into the bottom of four large ramekins or small ovenproof dishes.

Mix the cooled pasta with the whipped cream, then stir in the caster sugar to taste. Spoon the mixture into the ramekins, over the peaches. Leave until quite cold.

Preheat the grill until very hot. Place a thick layer of demerara sugar all over the top of the creamed macaroni, then quickly grill the sugar until it has melted and caramelised. Chill the brulées lightly before serving.

HONEY & CARDAMOM MACARONI

Honey and cardamom make the most delightful aromatic flavourings for this macaroni pudding.

Serves 4

INGREDIENTS
120g/4oz macaroni
430ml/¾ pint full cream milk
3-4 tbsps clear honey, or to taste
1 tsp cardamom seeds, lightly
   ground
150ml/¼ pint crème fraîche
Grated lemon rind to decorate

Place the macaroni, milk and honey in a large pan and cook until the macaroni is soft. Stir frequently, being careful not to allow the milk to boil over. Draw the pan off the heat and stir in the ground cardamom seeds. Allow the macaroni to cool slightly, then stir in the crème fraîche. Pour into a serving dish and top with grated lemon rind before serving.

CREAMY MACARONI WITH APRICOT PUREE

A slightly sharp apricot purée makes an excellent sauce to serve with a dish of rich, sweet pasta.

Serves 4

INGREDIENTS
460g/1lb fresh apricots, or
   225g/8oz no-soak dried
   apricots
150ml/¼ pint water
Grated rind and juice of 1 lemon
120g/4oz caster sugar
175g/6oz macaroni
280ml/½ pint double cream

Prepare the apricot purée. Stone the apricots if using fresh, and place them in a pan with the water, lemon rind and juice.

Cover and simmer for about 10 minutes, or until soft. Press the fruit through a sieve or blend in a liquidiser or food processor until smooth. Add 60-90g/2-3oz of the caster sugar, or to taste, and a little extra water if necessary.

Whilst the apricots are cooking, bring a large pan of water to the boil. Add the macaroni and cook until just tender but still firm. Drain and rinse in boiling water, then drain again. Heat the cream gently with the remaining sugar, then add the cooked macaroni and toss well. Serve the pasta with the apricot purée marbled through it.

INDEX